GW00326458

Kiddiwalks
IN
CHESHIRE

◆◆◆◆◆◆◆◆◆◆◆◆◆◆◆◆◆◆◆◆◆◆◆◆◆◆◆◆◆◆

John and Anne Nuttall

COUNTRYSIDE BOOKS
NEWBURY BERKSHIRE

First published 2007
© John and Anne Nuttall, 2007

COUNTRYSIDE BOOKS
3 Catherine Road
Newbury, Berkshire

To view our complete range of books,
please visit us at
www.countrysidebooks.co.uk

ISBN 978 1 84674 026 8

For Heather, Elizabeth,
Samuel and John

Photographs by John Nuttall

Designed by Peter Davies, Nautilus Design
Produced through MRM Associates Ltd., Reading
Typeset by Jean Cussons Typesetting, Diss, Norfolk
Printed by Cambridge University Press

Contents ◆◆◆◆◆◆◆◆◆◆◆◆◆◆◆◆◆◆

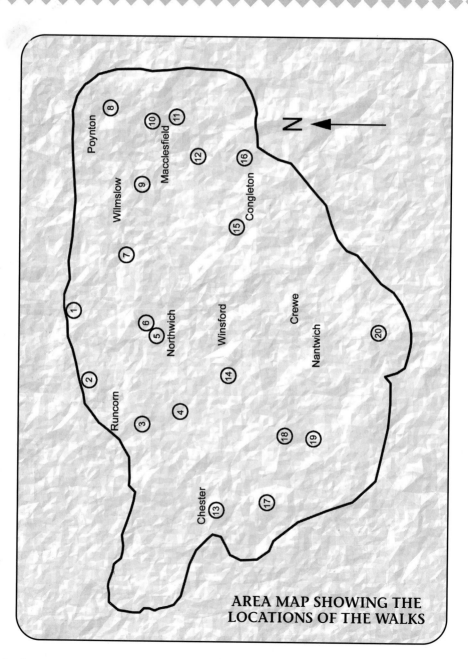

AREA MAP SHOWING THE
LOCATIONS OF THE WALKS

Contents

PUBLISHER'S NOTE
We hope that you obtain considerable enjoyment from this book; great care has been taken in its preparation. Although at the time of publication all routes followed public rights of way or permitted paths, diversion orders can be made and permissions withdrawn.

We cannot, of course, be held responsible for such diversion orders and any inaccuracies in the text which result from these or any other changes to the routes nor any damage which might result from walkers trespassing on private property. We are anxious though that all details covering the walks are kept up to date and would therefore welcome information from readers which would be relevant to future editions.

The simple sketch maps that accompany the walk in this book are based on notes made by the author whilst checking out the routes on the ground. However, for the benefit of a proper map, we do recommend that you purchase the relevant Ordnance Survey sheet covering your walk. The Ordnance Survey maps are widely available, especially through booksellers and local newsagents.

Introduction

With our first child we started with a pram. We dragged it down muddy tracks and across the moors and, when winter came, hauled it through snowdrifts too. Very soon the pram was a wreck. Then came a papoose carrier bringing wilder and more remote places within reach. Most friends, however, viewed our family walks with a mixture of pity and admiration. 'You are good, taking your children with you,' they said. But perhaps the unspoken suggestion was that we would put our children off for life. How wrong they were! Both are still enthusiastic walkers, together with their wives and now the next generation as well. After all, family walks are even easier when grandpa is available to carry one of the children.

So what are the essentials to ensure the children will enjoy their day out? The answer is to keep them interested. Things to balance on, jump off, or crawl through are far more interesting than views. Climbing rocks is much more attractive than the steps at the side, while splashing through puddles is more fun than walking round them. And storytelling isn't just for bedtime. The tale of the Three Little Pigs has made many a mile pass for us when young legs got tired, while sending one of them ahead to hide round the corner means suddenly those legs aren't tired after all.

Cheshire is not somewhere that springs instantly to mind when planning exciting walks, but the county is full of surprises with extensive woodland, parkland and even some worthy summits. Lyme Park has an untamed wildness about its moorland fringe while Tatton Park was one of the first landscape gardens and, in both, there are herds of deer roaming freely. Anderton Nature Park adjoins that triumph of Victorian engineering the Anderton Boat Lift, and at Chester you can combine walking the historic walls with a visit to its unique double row of shops. Woodland is well represented with Delamere Forest, which is big enough to get lost in, and Little Budworth, which is often quite deserted. Then there's Alderley Edge, with its legend of the wizard and a mysterious door in the hillside. Gawsworth is one of those delightful Cheshire villages with fields, a canal and an area of ancient peat moss. For more canalside rambles there's Audlem and Lymm Dam, while even more water will be found at Aldford on the River Dee. Brereton Heath has an old sand quarry lake and Marbury Country Park a stately mere, while Moore Nature Reserve boasts woodpeckers and owls in a woodland and lakeside setting. But what about those summits? From Frodsham Hill there's a bird's-eye view of the Mersey Estuary, while the ramparts of Maiden Castle are easy to scale. The cave beneath Raw Head is big, mysterious and never to be forgotten, while at Tegg's Nose you start and finish on a summit with hardly any ascent at all. But if hills are your passion, The Cloud is a mountain in miniature, and the climb up to White Nancy provides the most challenging route in the book.

We hope you enjoy these walks as much as we have for, above all, walking with children is fun!

John and Anne Nuttall

Cheshire's glorious countryside seen from Kerridge Hill.

Lymm Dam

Jumping with the Squirrels

Near Lymm Dam.

You could go for a walk without the children getting dirty, but what would be the point? It's simply that the most enjoyable activities have a habit of getting their clothes messy. On this route the high spot for us was rolling acorns down an eroded sandstone outcrop, sliding down to fetch them and then climbing back up to do it all over again. But there's more to Lymm Dam than just acorns. There are fallen trees to balance along and jump off. There are tame squirrels that even like bananas. The lake itself is a surprisingly large stretch of water in the middle of one of Cheshire's up-market towns, and then there are the brightly painted boats cruising the Bridgewater Canal. But do bring some spare clothes so you don't have to get the car valeted afterwards!

Lymm Dam

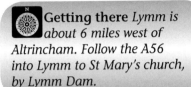

Getting there *Lymm is about 6 miles west of Altrincham. Follow the A56 into Lymm to St Mary's church, by Lymm Dam.*

Length of walk 3½ miles.
Time About 3 hours
Terrain Easy paths and a few steps.
Start/Parking Turn up Crouchley Lane, in the centre of Lymm, and park behind Lymm church in the small free car park by St Mary's church hall (GR 684867).
Map OS Explorer 276 Bolton, Wigan & Warrington.
Refreshments Lymm offers a choice of pubs and the Golden Fleece has a beer garden by the canal. There is a picnic site by Lymm Dam, which you pass at both the beginning and the end of the walk.

The Walk

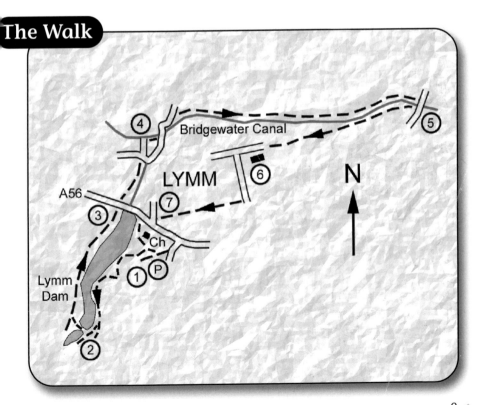

Kiddiwalks in Cheshire

1

1 Walk past the 'Welcome to Lymm Dam' notice and keep straight on beside the bridleway, then fork right along the surfaced path. This leads amongst the trees and continues high above the lake, through a picnic area where you should see grey squirrels.

2 Go down the steps and cross the pretty little bridge above a waterfall, which links the Upper and the Middle Dam. Now turn right and continue round the lake, following the waterside path through the trees, with lovely views across to Lymm church.

3 Taking care, cross straight over the busy A56 by the arched dam and continue down The Dingle, following the shady path beside Bradley Brook to emerge in the centre of Lymm by the Lower Dam. Then turn left up Bridgewater Street to the Bridgewater Canal.

4 Turn right beside the brightly-painted boats but, before you cross Lymm Bridge, look down into the square to see the ancient market cross. The walk now continues along the towpath for about a mile to Oughtrington Bridge.

◆ Fun Things to See and Do ◆

The woodland around **Lymm Dam** is home to a large number of grey squirrels, especially in the picnic area. It is also very good for birdwatching so keep a look out for the nuthatch, treecreeper, lesser spotted woodpecker and heron. You may even be lucky enough to glimpse a kingfisher, for they nest here. Birds seen on the lake include mallards, coots, moorhens, great crested grebes, pochards, mandarin, muscovy and tufted ducks, Canada geese and teal. In autumn the oaks are laden with acorns and the horse chestnuts with conkers.

In Lymm village you pass Little Jo's Toy Shop and friendly boaters on the canal give cheery waves. The highlight of our day was the sandstone cliff below the church for a final play on the eroded rocks, but the children did get very dirty! St Mary's church clock strikes the hour and quarters so the children can listen to it to tell the time.

Lymm Dam

5 Here you can show the children where the tow ropes have bitten deeply into the brickwork. Then cross the canal and immediately double-back along the shaded bridleway, which gives good views of Oughtrington church – look for horseshoe prints on the ground.

6 Meeting the road, go past the school, then turn left up Orchard Avenue. At the top of the road turn right on the higher path and keep straight on, with a choice of either the path or the field. Then, joining the road, head for the church.

7 Cross back over the A56 and walk beside Lymm Dam beneath a sculpted sandstone outcrop (excellent scrambling), then continue along the board walk before climbing back up the steps to the picnic area.

◆ Background Notes ◆

Lymm Dam was formed in 1824 when the new turnpike road from Warrington to Stockport, the present A56, dammed Bradley Brook and flooded the marsh near the church. The park was originally landscaped by the first Lord Leverhulme who planted the Lombardy poplars, the oaks, beech, ash and sycamores, and also created the lakeside paths. Bradley Brook flows from the Upper Dam into the Middle Dam, down through The Dingle and into the Lower Dam. **Lymm Heritage Trail** has several interesting explanatory boards giving information about the wildlife, woodland, birds and the geology of Lymm Dam. It is thought that the sandstone outcrops in the valley were shaped by meltwater at the end of the Ice Age.

The **grey squirrels** are incomers and were introduced into this country from North America in the 19th century.

James Brindley's **Bridgewater Canal** was the first canal to be built in England and this section, joining Worsley to Runcorn, was constructed around 1770.

St Mary's church dates back to the 10th century, though it has been rebuilt four times. The present building was erected in 1851.

2

Moore Nature Reserve

Walking Under Water

Walking through a flower-filled meadow.

Watching silent, khaki-clad figures setting off towards the woodland, wetland and reedbeds of Moore Nature Reserve you can tell straight away that it's either the site of an SAS exercise or a birdwatchers' heaven. Well, it's the latter, for among the trees you will find enthusiasts peering intently from the slit-like windows of the numerous bird hides that overlook the lakes. Here telescopes, binoculars, and cameras with enormous lenses are the order of the day. Did you know there are three different kinds of woodpecker and five species of owl? At Moore Nature Reserve you are in with a chance of seeing them all. And if the kids find birds boring, there's always a muddy puddle to jump in, or just tell them they are walking under water, for one path follows the bed of the old Runcorn to Latchford Canal.

Moore Nature Reserve

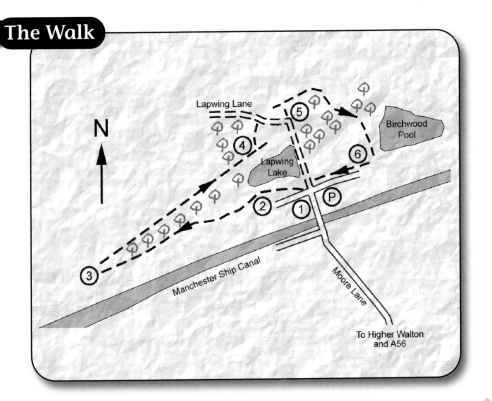

Getting there *Moore Nature Reserve is 3 miles south-west of Warrington. Turn off the A56 at Higher Walton traffic lights towards Moore, then go right down Moore Lane and cross the swing bridge to the Lapwing Lane crossroads.*

Length of walk 2 miles.
Time At least 2 hours
Terrain Good paths, but not suitable for pushchairs, though you could do the wheelchair path instead.

Start/Parking Park on the right near the end of Lapwing Lane (GR 578855).
Map OS Explorer 276 Bolton, Wigan & Warrington. You will find a map of the Reserve in a box by entrance.
Refreshments Take a picnic. The nearest pub is the Red Lion in Moore.

The Walk

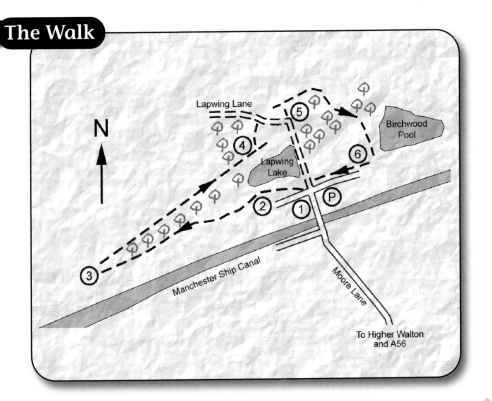

Kiddiwalks in Cheshire

◆◆◆*2*◆◆◆◆◆◆◆◆◆◆◆◆◆◆◆◆◆◆◆◆◆◆◆◆◆◆◆◆◆◆◆

① From the crossroads follow the Nature Trail left, up the grassy bank to a bird hide facing Lapwing Lake. How many different birds can you see? Go up the steps and continue through the trees to a seat overlooking the lake.

② Now turn left down into the gorse-filled Hillcrest Quarry, past several small ponds, and continue to a footbridge.

③ Turn right along the old canal bed, then continue on a surfaced path past a couple more hides. Are the birds on the lake the same as the birds in the fields?

④ After climbing up onto the towpath, turn left across a

◆ Fun Things to See and Do ◆

Children will enjoy finding the hides and looking through the windows at the unsuspecting birds on Lapwing Lake. There is a new hide overlooking recently planted Forestry Commission land on the restored landfill site, while another hide gives a close up view of a Bird Feeding Station. You will also encounter butterflies, dragonflies and lots of wild flowers in season, including orchids, and in the summer months one of the best displays we've ever seen of bird's-foot trefoil.

The walk goes along the bed of the disused Runcorn to Latchford Canal where you can still see the **sandstone canal walls**. It doesn't seem possible that enormous boats, known as Mersey Sailing Flats, once came this way, travelling between Liverpool and Manchester.

Gulliver's Theme Park, suitable for children aged 2–13, is only about 5 miles away on the outskirts of Warrington. There are rides, shows and attractions, which are all free once you have paid to get in. Telephone: 01925 444888; www.gulliversfun.co.uk

reedbed on a board walk. Reaching Lapwing Lane turn right. (If the children are tired continue along the lane, back to the start.)

5 Go left at the bend and past a Bird Feeding Station. How many different woodland birds can you spot? What are they eating? Turn right at the T-junction and follow

the path into the trees past the Plague Pit and continue into mature woodland, then keep straight on across the meadow, by Birchwood Pool.

6 Climb the steps by the signpost and follow the gravelled path, then head across the meadow back to Lapwing Lane.

Birchwood Pool.

◆ Background Notes ◆

Moore Nature Reserve has almost 200 acres of woodland, meadow, lakes and ponds. The bird life is very varied. There are also many different varieties of wild flowers so don't forget flower books, bird books and binoculars. From Lapwing Hide look out for kingfishers, great crested grebes and wintering ducks and from the Feeding Station you may see nuthatches, great spotted woodpeckers and marsh and willow tits. More information on Moore Nature Reserve can be found at www.wrg.co.uk/moorenaturereserve

Lapwing Lake was created in 1988 by the extraction of clay used as a lining for Arpley Landfill Site. The walk goes along the edge of the landfill which will eventually all be restored to woodland and grassland. Show the children the completed areas where thousands of young trees have been planted.

The **Manchester Ship Canal** is crossed on your way to the start and you may be lucky enough to see the swing bridge open. **Hillcrest Quarry** was created when sand was dumped here in the 1900s during the digging of the Ship Canal, then around 90 years later the area was quarried and the high grade sand used commercially. The quarry was made into a hilly area and now the ponds support water voles, dragonflies and even the great crested newt, which is protected.

The **Plague Pit** is a meadow where canal workers were buried after a plague epidemic occurred while they were digging the canal. The old **Runcorn to Latchford Canal** opened in 1804 to carry trade vessels, known as Mersey Sailing Flats. This bypassed a section of the River Mersey, but its use declined when the Ship Canal opened and this stretch was breached in the 1970s.

3

Frodsham Hill

Hillfort and Glaciers

The view from Frodsham Hill.

'Prominent rocky situation with magnificent view over the Mersey Estuary' might have been the estate agent's description. And the asking price? Just £8. Of course prices have risen rather a lot since this valuation for Frodsham appeared in the Domesday Book, but this tree-cloaked sandstone hill, topped by an Iron Age hillfort, is still a delightful place for a walk. Or how about a run? Just pretend you are the attacking army charging up the slope towards your enemies among the pine trees. Then, when everyone arrives gasping at the top, it's easy to explain why the fort was built on a summit carved out by the Ice Age.

Kiddiwalks in Cheshire

3

Getting there *Frodsham is situated just off the M56, junction 12, on the A56. From the B5152 turn up Manley Road and then go right along Simons Lane, following signs to Forest Hills Hotel.*

Length of walk 3 miles (adventurous) or 1 mile (easy)
Time Up to 3 hours.
Terrain Clear paths above steep drops, but the longer walk has steep ups and downs and lots of steps. **Warning** The walks follow the top of a steep sandstone escarpment and there are unfenced cliffs so children should be closely supervised.
Start/Parking The Sandstone Trail, Beacon Hill free car park (GR 519766).
Map OS Explorer 267 Northwich & Delamere Forest.
Refreshments Take a picnic to enjoy at one of the tremendous viewpoints.

◆ Fun Things to See and Do ◆

The first lot of steps is called '**Baker's Dozen**'. Count them and see if the children can think why there are 13 not 12. Although we've been up **Jacob's Ladder** it's not suitable for anyone unaccustomed to rock scrambling.

The **views over the Mersey Basin** and towards Helsby Hill are spectacular and an information board by the viewpoint seat explains the geology of the landscape. The children can look out for rounded boulders in the field walls, which were carried here during the Ice Age.

In autumn the children can scuff through the leaves and hunt for fungi. In all seasons there are trees to identify. The youngsters can also examine all the different layers on the **red sandstone cliffs** and feel how the rock is simply sand stuck together. Where did the sand come from?

Finally comes the **topograph**, which points out the curve of the Widnes–Runcorn Bridge, the distant Winter Hill and the Welsh mountains.

The Walk

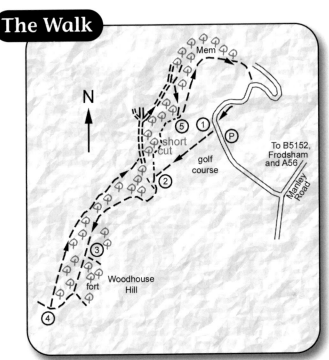

The *longer walk* turns left down the wooden steps to Dunsdale Hollow. Jacob's Ladder lies to the right, a rather intimidating cliff scramble which was once the only way up. Staying on the level you now follow the Sandstone Trail beneath a cliff and up the rocky steps of Abraham's Leap, then continue along the top of the wood.

3 Reaching a viewpoint seat, leave the Sandstone Trail and keep straight on along the top of the cliffs, beneath Woodhouse Hill, the site of the Iron Age hillfort. Meeting a fence by open ground a waymark points right and a little path slants steeply down through the trees.

1 Turn right out of Beacon Hill car park then, in about 50 yards, go left along the Sandstone Trail. A narrow footpath leads down to the golf course then heads straight across the fairway to the escarpment edge.

2 *For the short walk* turn right along the top of the steep slope where Sandstone Trail waymarks point you on past a viewpoint seat, below old quarries and eroded sandstone cliffs, to join the *longer walk* at point 5.

4 At the bottom of Woodhouse Hill you turn right and follow the easy path along the bottom of the wood for about a mile, then climb the steps beside a stone wall. Staying by the wall, go gently downhill, then turn right along

Kiddiwalks in Cheshire

the track past some houses. Take the next fork right, then in 50 yards go right on a footpath which turns steeply uphill. Wooden steps now lead up to an old quarry where you turn left and rejoin the short walk.

5 The path continues through the trees to the war memorial and the Mersey View topograph. Then take the broad grassy path, which heads away from the edge to the left of the Forest Hills Hotel fence. This leads out through the war memorial gates where you turn right along Simons Lane, back to the car park.

◆ Background Notes ◆

The small market town of Frodsham is the start of the **Sandstone Trail**, a long-distance footpath, which links Beacon Hill with Grindley Brook, near Whitchurch. The Trail follows the Central Cheshire Ridge, which is made from sandstone formed in the Triassic period, 300 million years ago. The first settlers at Frodsham were Anglo-Saxons from Mercia whose leader was called Frod, while ham means homestead or hamm, a promontory extending into marshland.

Woodhouse Hill is the most northerly of the seven Iron Age hillforts that lie on the sandstone ridge. The fort would have had a commanding view over the plain and would have housed several families in huts behind the defensive stone and earth ramparts.

Frodsham Hill Wood, which includes some ancient woodland, is now owned and managed by the Woodland Trust and is mainly deciduous woodland composed of oak, beech, birch, holly and rowan.

The views on this walk are outstanding and you look out across the tidal marshes and reedbeds to the **Mersey Basin**, which in 1894 was reclaimed for farmland and industry.

The war memorial stands on **Overton Hill** at 365 ft, which was once the site of Mersey View pavilion and pleasure grounds.

4

Delamere Forest

Navigating in the Woods

Strolling through the forest.

The biggest expanse of woodland in Cheshire, Delamere, is a child-friendly forest. From easy paths and tracks for pushchairs, to narrower paths that meander through the trees and even excitingly mysterious paths, where every twist and turn is a constant surprise, there is something for everyone. Delamere is a great place to introduce children to map reading and when their skills have improved, why not try winter? After snow has fallen and paths and tracks have disappeared beneath a white blanket, all places begin to look alike. It is then that the signs come in handy, for helpfully every junction has a post with a number. But if you have an old map the lake will come as a surprise. Is this evidence of global warming? No, it's just that experts are recreating the ancient Blakemere Moss. So, if your navigation is a bit rusty, just keep the lake on your left and you won't go far wrong!

Kiddiwalks in Cheshire

4

Getting there *Delamere Forest Park, 6 miles west of Northwich, is signed from the A556 and Linmere Lodge is off the B5152, beyond Delamere station.*

Length of walk 2¾ miles.
Time About 2½ hours.
Terrain Good paths, very pushchair friendly.
Start/Parking Linmere Lodge Visitor Centre car park, small charge, toilets (GR 549704).

Map OS Explorer 267 Northwich & Delamere Forest, but the Delamere Forest Guide, available from Linmere Lodge Visitor Centre, is the best map for this walk.
Refreshments The café and gift shop at the visitor centre is very pleasant and they welcome children, providing high chairs and a corner for drawing and looking at storybooks. There are lots of picnic tables and the ones at Linmere Lodge are even under cover.

The Walk

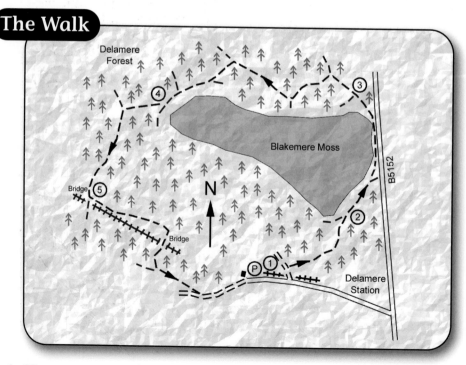

Delamere Forest

1 From the Linmere Lodge car park, turn left along the approach road, then go left again over the railway bridge to the start of the Blakemere Trail. Now look for the red waymarks and follow the broad path through the trees past 'Go Ape'. Are you tempted to have a go?

2 Reaching Blakemere Moss the Trail goes right beside the shallow lake and you follow the little path which stays near the water's edge. Just before the road, the red waymarks point on beside the lake, but if bumping a pushchair over tree roots is too much like hard work continue up to the

◆ Fun Things to See and Do ◆

The **Blakemere Trail** is waymarked with red-topped posts and the children will enjoy looking out for the next marker. There is also a shorter, green trail and two waymarked cycle trails. Some of the posts mark more than one trail, so the younger children can point to the different colours. The Delamere Forest Guide map makes a good introduction to map reading. The waymark posts at the path junction are all numbered to correspond with the map, so getting lost is almost impossible (now there's a challenge!).

Delamere is a working forest where you may well see piles of logs and neatly sawn tree stumps. Show the children how you can tell the age of a tree by counting the rings. At all times of the year grey squirrels can be spotted in the woods.

The Trail crosses the **Chester to Manchester Railway**, which was completed in 1869, and as the trains run every hour you may be lucky enough to see one and even get a toot from the engine driver if you wave.

The Linmere Lodge café windows look out on an array of bird tables to encourage the **forest birds**, which include the goldcrest, nuthatch, blue tit and coal tit, and of course the chaffinch.

4

road and turn left along the pavement.

3 Joining a forest track the Trail keeps straight on, up Hunger Hill, then turns left at the T-junction. Now go gently down, only to climb again before finally descending to the main path. The forest track leads round the far end of the mere where the water is much shallower, forming a mosaic in which birch scrub is regenerating.

4 At a signpost the Blakemere Trail goes right to join forces with the Wheelchair Easi Trail and climbs the hill to a T-junction where you turn left along the

Finding the way.

Sandstone Trail, which is marked with a bootprint waymark. The attractive path leads through sweet chestnut trees and you keep straight on, past a tree stump that has been carved into a seat, then fork left to the railway bridge. What does the road sign mean?

5 Don't cross the bridge, but turn left. A red waymark points you down the track and across the next bridge. Now follow the track, which climbs to the edge of the wood and leads back to Linmere Lodge.

◆ Background Notes ◆

The name **Delamere** comes from the French and means 'of the mere'. At one time the forest stretched all the way from the River Mersey to Nantwich. This huge medieval forest of Mara and Mondrum was created by the Normans in the 11th century. Later, Delamere became a royal hunting ground for deer and wild boar, but these days you don't have to be a king, everyone's welcome.

The **Blakemere** Trail is well signed and uses quiet paths and tracks, which encircle Blakemere Moss. The moss, which was scooped out by an Ice Age glacier, was drained by French prisoners during the Napoleonic Wars. About ten years ago the trees covering this boggy area were clear felled and the land flooded to destroy the surface vegetation and re-establish a wildlife-rich wetland area, recreating the ancient Blakemere Moss. The water in the mere is too acid to support much pond life.

At the beginning of the Trail you pass 'Go Ape' where children and adults can get from tree to tree via an assortment of rope bridges and Tarzan swings. Then zip slides deliver you back to the forest floor. Children must be at least 10 years old and over 4 ft 7 ins to use this equipment, but you may prefer to try orienteering where at least everyone's feet are firmly on the ground.

As you stroll round the forest there are views to the mast on **Eddisbury Hill**, which is the site of an ancient Iron Age fort.

5

Anderton Nature Park

Flowers, Insects and Victorian Engineering

The fun waymarks in the nature park.

Dragonflies are usually difficult for children to watch as, with a flash of silver, they are soon away. But you can't miss the dragonfly in Anderton Nature Park, for it's about five feet high and made of wood. This novel idea illustrates the creatures of a delightful lime-rich area and, as well as insects, there are many lovely flowers, among them marsh orchids, fragrant orchids, dog roses, ragged robin and common centaury. So put binoculars and a flower book into your rucksack and you'll have a great day out. Then, when you get back, there's the Anderton Boat Lift to visit. This miracle of Victorian engineering is now working again with boats being lowered to the river below. Truly a memorable end to an enjoyable walk.

Anderton Nature Park

Getting there *Anderton Nature Park is 1 mile north of Northwich. Follow signs to the Anderton Boat Lift from the A533.*

Length of walk 1 mile.
Time Up to 1 hour.
Terrain Broad paths, suitable for pushchairs.

Start/Parking Anderton Boat Lift car park, small charge, toilets at the visitor centre (GR 649754).
Map OS Explorer 267 Northwich & Delamere Forest.
Refreshments The visitor centre, the Anderton Marina Restaurant and the Stanley Arms, next to the Boat Lift, which welcomes children. The park is also well supplied with picnic tables.

The Walk

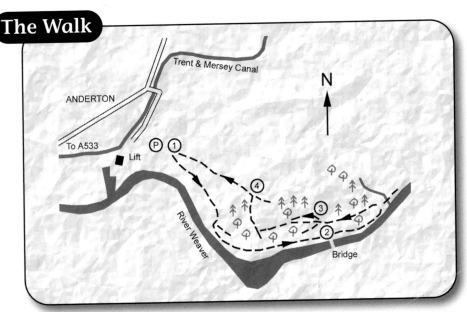

1 From the far side of the Anderton Boat Lift car park, take the path through the dragonfly gates into the park. Continue to the signpost and follow the Wild Flower Trail downhill to the Dragonfly Pond, then continue along the lower path beside the River Weaver and past the rifle range.

Kiddiwalks in Cheshire

5

◆ Fun Things to See and Do ◆

After looking at the **Anderton Nature Park** map, which is a real work of art, the fun begins straight away as you pass between two huge dragonflies, which form a gate. The **Dragonfly Pond**, with its mid-pond sculpture, has an excellent information board that tells you all about the damselflies and dragonflies you may see. They do so well because the water is too salty for fish and frogs, which would eat their young.

Here you will find the first of the **trail markers** showing the flowers and plants to look for nearby, helpfully including their height and flowering time. You pass lots of these trail posts on the walk. Younger children can count the number of sides on the markers; most have three but some are square. By the riverbank you will find plants like the great willowherb, while in spring the air is full of the garlic scent of ramsons. There are also buddleia bushes, often covered with butterflies in summer for they love the purple flowers. The ground sloping down to the river is a wooded ash bank where you will see lots of teasels. Look at their teeth – they were once used to raise the nap during cloth manufacture. Higher up is the lime waste where lime-loving plants such as bird's-foot trefoil grow. You can also hunt for the rare fragrant orchid, which the children can identify by its scent (it's the only orchid in the park with a scent). There are violets in the damp woodland glades and don't miss the pennyroyal whose leaves smell of mint.

Children can have fun balancing along **park sculptures** and climbing on the caterpillar's back. Short wooden posts mark path junctions, which are great for playing statues.

Finish off with a visit to the **Anderton Boat Lift** and its **visitor centre** where you can see the exhibition, take a ride on the lift, have a cup of tea and treat the kids to that promised ice cream.

2 Reaching the new black and white Carden's Ferry Bridge, don't cross but continue along the riverbank for another 200 yards. Now you turn sharp left on a main path, which climbs the hill and continues up through Marshalls Wood to a crossroads.

3 Turning right, you now head back to the Anderton Boat Lift car park through silver birch woodland. Go right at the next junction and cross a grassy area, then go right again and follow the path, which curves uphill.

4 Reaching a signpost, turn left and keep straight on past the sculptures, which are good for climbing on, back to the car park and the canal.

Admiring the dragonfly sculpture.

◆ Background Notes ◆

Anderton Nature Park is an industrial wasteland that has been magically transformed into a wildlife heaven. In the early 1900s the lime waste from the soda industry was dumped here behind ash clinker walls, then the mixture gradually solidified and soon became colonised by lime-loving plants. The salt, lime and ash clinker create different habitats, which means that some unusual plants, not normally found locally, grow here. The nature park, which is bounded by the River Weaver, has been managed to create wetland, woodland and calcareous grassland, which encourages water birds, woodland birds, butterflies and moths. June, July and August are the best months to visit the park.

The restored **Anderton Boat Lift** was built in 1875 to move barges the 50 feet between the River Weaver and the Trent & Mersey Canal. It was a world-first triumph of Victorian engineering and is now in full working order, a major tourist attraction.

6
Marbury Country Park

Ghost Beside the Mere

Exploring the winding paths.

There aren't many country parks that are haunted, but the one at Marbury is. And this is no ordinary, chain-clanking ghost, for the White Lady was an Egyptian princess. The hall in which she came to live with her lover is no more, but she has been seen strolling across the lawns of her once stately home in its lovely setting beside Budworth Mere. Every winter the lake is host to golden eye and greylag geese, while among the woodland the great spotted woodpecker can be seen. So, as the children explore the twisting woodland paths or experimentally dip their feet in the lake, tell them the ghost isn't a scary ghost, she just liked living here very, very much.

Marbury Country Park

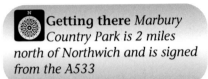

Getting there *Marbury Country Park is 2 miles north of Northwich and is signed from the A533*

Length of walk 1½ miles.
Time At least 2 hours.
Terrain Good paths, suitable for pushchairs. The steps can be easily bumped down or avoided by heading straight for the mere.

Start/Parking The Country Park car park, small charge, toilets (GR 653764).
Map OS Explorer 267 Northwich & Delamere Forest.
Refreshments There are no refreshments in the Country Park, but you will find lots of picnic tables and there may well be an ice cream van around.

The Walk

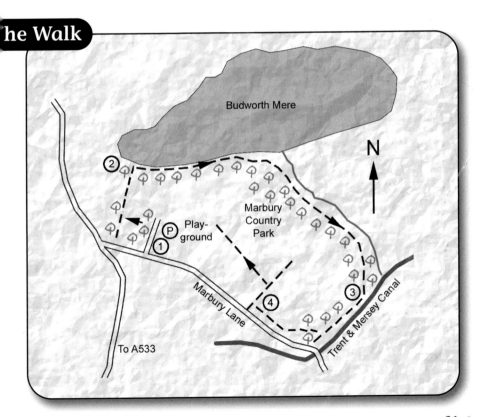

Kiddiwalks in Cheshire

6

1 From the car park entrance, cross the road into the arboretum and, with a choice of paths, stroll through the trees to join the Carriage Drive. Turn right across the grassy area, the site of Marbury Hall, and go down the steps to the bird hide at the water's edge.

◆ Fun Things to See and Do ◆

 Marbury Arboretum has a large number of tree species and the carved wooden posts will help the children identify stately conifers and unusual trees from all round the world. The carriage drive has the original iron gate and railings, but the grand hall is long gone. Perhaps the children could imagine what it would have been like to have lived here then.

There will be ducks on the mere begging for food so a bird book and binoculars would be useful. One hide overlooks the reedbed of **Budworth Mere**, where you may see great crested grebes or hear the reed warbler, and there is another by a feeding station for woodland birds. Before the days of refrigerators, ice from the mere and the pond was used. The ice was cut up and stored in the ice house, which had a deep pit lined by a double wall of bricks with a space between and originally it had a domed roof. The ice house was shaded from the sun by the surrounding yew trees. Amazingly, if the ice was mixed with salt it would keep for up to two years.

From the lakeshore you look over to **Great Budworth**, which, as well as having a pub, also has a real dairy ice cream farm (www.icecreamfarm.co.uk).

Marbury Country Park has an unheated **outdoor swimming pool**, which, though for members only, admits the public if it is not too busy. There is also a small children's pool. An **adventure playground** is always fun and the one at Marbury is set in pleasant surroundings, though it is not suitable for very young children.

Marbury Country Park

2 Turning right, follow the path beside Budworth Mere and above a boathouse, to an old slipway with a view of Great Budworth church. Continuing through the woods, look out for a fenced brick-lined pit and a pond, both with chilly connections. After visiting the Woodland Bird Hide take the broader path through Big Wood, which passes a wonderful carved seat. How many animals can the children find?

3 Reaching the Trent & Mersey Canal, don't cross the black and white footbridge, but continue through the trees. Keep right at the fork and walk through Black Wood.

4 Arriving at a main track, which leads out to Marbury Lane, turn right. In about 100 yards go left across the grazing field. Continue through the trees to Lime Avenue, then turn left to finish off the walk in the adventure playground.

◆ Background Notes ◆

The 200 acre **Marbury Country Park** has a lovely setting beside Budworth Mere. 'Marbury' means a fortified dwelling by a lake and this was the name of the family that settled here in the 12th century. There have been three halls at Marbury. The most recent was built in the 1850s and was modelled on the French chateau at Fontainebleau. After the family left, it became a country club, then, during the Second World War, the house was requisitioned by the army and used as a prisoner of war camp. Though Marbury Hall itself was demolished in 1968, the two long avenues of lime trees are remnants of the original parkland.

This part of Cheshire is famous for its salt and it was in Marbury's **Big Wood** that the first rock salt in Britain was discovered in 1670 when people were prospecting for coal. Five years later the first rock salt mine was dug and then the salt was carried by packhorses all over the country.

Tatton Park

Architect-Designed Landscape

The fine temple in Tatton Park.

Owning several thousand acres and not having a garden is surprising. But in the 18th century many of the landed gentry had just a great park sweeping right up to the front door. Then came Humphry Repton, and at Tatton Park he gave them not only a most attractive formal garden, but a garden outside as well, for the woods, trees and wide open spaces were his creation as the very first landscape gardener. Such men plan with a vision and only his children's children would see how the little saplings became stately beech trees complementing the wide open spaces around a mile-long mere, with red and fallow deer roaming freely. Youngsters can run wild here and afterwards, when they're comfortably tired, you could always take in the formal garden too. And if you belong to the National Trust, entry is absolutely free!

◆◆◆◆◆◆◆◆◆◆◆◆◆◆◆◆◆◆◆◆◆◆◆◆◆◆◆◆◆◆◆◆◆◆◆◆◆◆◆

Getting there *Tatton Park is 12 miles south of Manchester. The main way into the park is signed from the A50 and A556 and there is another entrance, just to the north of Knutsford.*

Length of walk 2½ miles.
Time Allow a couple of hours, plus extra time for the playground.
Terrain Easy going with mostly grassy paths. The walk is not suitable for pushchairs, but you will find lots of tarmac tracks in the park that are.

Start/Parking Tatton Park main car park by the house (GR 744816). Entry charge for cars, including National Trust members. Toilets in stable yard. Note Tatton Park is closed on Mondays in winter. Telephone 01625 534400 for opening times of the mansion, Old Hall and Home Farm. See also www.tattonpark.org.uk
Map OS Explorer 268 Wilmslow, Macclesfield & Congleton.

The Walk

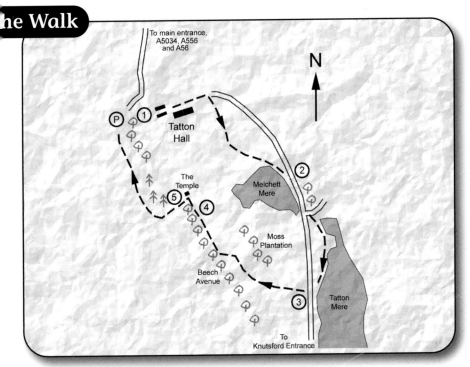

A free map of the park is supplied on entry.
Refreshments There is a restaurant in the stable yard and also ice cream vans in the park at busy times of the year.

1 Walk through the stable yard, past the entrance to the gardens, then continue to the mansion and out into the park. Stay near the garden perimeter fence for about 200 yards, then head across the grass. As you crest the rise, Melchett Mere comes into view. Go down to the water's edge, then walk leftwards round the lake.

2 Joining Knutsford Drive, follow this to the track junction and fork left, then head across

◆ Fun Things to See and Do ◆

Both **red deer and fallow deer** are to be found in Tatton Park. In spring the deer shed their antlers and in the autumn the rutting season begins with the bellowing of the stags, quite an alarming sound. The park contains a variety of **wildlife habitats**, including woodland and wetland. There is plenty of bird life throughout the year so a pair of binoculars will be helpful. In spring the migrating birds arrive and waterfowl nest and breed. There are large flocks of Canada geese, which honk loudly as they fly overhead in formation, while, in the summer, swifts, swallows and martins are plentiful.

There is a large **play area** next to the car park, which is suitable for pre-school children and up to 12 years of age.

A calendar of events offers lots of activities at Tatton Park throughout the year. The **house and gardens** are open to the public (free to NT members), with the **garden maze** a must for children. There is the **Home Farm**, stocked with breeds that would have been found here in the 1930s, and the **Old Hall**, which recreates life as it would have formerly been lived at Tatton. All of these attractions are extra to the car park charge, but the delights of the park are free.

the grass to a kissing gate and walk beside Tatton Mere. The path continues along a raised embankment, fun to balance on, heading towards the distant tower of Knutsford church.

3 When the lakeside path nears Knutsford Drive, cross the tarmac and follow the clear path across the rough grass. The path climbs above Moss Plantation, a secluded haunt of the deer, then, heading leftwards, you reach Beech Avenue, a great place to scuff through autumn leaves.

4 Drawing level with the end of Melchett Mere, watch for a fenced enclosure by a clump of lime trees, 50 yards to the right, which hides the ice house. Now head for the monument in the formal gardens. The ha-ha comes as a surprise – can the children guess why this hidden ditch is here?

5 Turning left to a kissing gate, you cross the field to a tall kissing gate in the corner. Why is it so high? Then a path leads through the trees and across the grass to the children's playground.

Fallow deer roam freely in the park.

◆ Background Notes ◆

Tatton Park was developed as a farming community and deer park in the Middle Ages. The Old Hall, a medieval manor house, was built at the end of this period. The wealthy Egerton family acquired Tatton in late Tudor times and turned it into a landscaped park, building the neo-classical house around 1800. The mansion encompasses splendid staterooms, a Victorian kitchen, family memorabilia, fine art and furniture collections, together with 50 acres of gardens. The stable yard houses a restaurant and gift shops. You can wander at will through the park so the walk can be lengthened or shortened to suit both the children and the weather.

The original **Tatton Mere** was formed when the monks of Mobberley Priory dammed the River Lily 800 years ago.

Melchett Mere was created by subsidence in the 1920s due to brine pumping nearby. It was named by Lord Egerton, with tongue in cheek, after Lord Melchett, the chairman of the salt company.

Beech Avenue was planted in the 1730s and some of the original trees are still standing.

It is worth going down to look inside the **ice house** where ice from the meres was stored to preserve and prepare food in spring and summer before refrigerators were invented. In 1883 a new ice house was built nearer the hall and this one was used as a silo to preserve grass for winter fodder.

The monument in Tatton Park garden is a **classical temple**, commissioned by Wilbraham Egerton in 1820.

8

Lyme Park

Roaming with the Deer

All set for an adventure.

Lyme Park is one of those places that never seems to be crowded and in October, with twilight fast approaching and stags roaring their challenges, the moor can acquire the remote and wild atmosphere of a Scottish glen. Here you will find the stately 18th century Lyme Hall, built in the style of an Italian palace, and then there's Lyme Cage. Looking every inch a sinister prison, this was used as a banqueting house and a viewpoint for ladies to watch the hunt. Although named because it looked like a birdcage, it was also used as a temporary prison for poachers – before that they were simply shot! The Lantern is another tower set in the woods, while roaming freely in the park are herds of red and fallow deer. But do save some energy for the end of the walk as that's where you'll find the swings and slides.

Kiddiwalks in Cheshire

Getting there *Take the A6 between Stockport and Whaley Bridge. Turn off southwards for Lyme Park 6 miles from Stockport and ½ mile west of Disley. There is a railway station at Disley and local buses pass the park entrance.*

Length of walk 3 miles.
Time Allow about 2 hours, plus extra time for the playground.
Terrain Good paths, but lots of ups and downs.

Start/Parking National Trust main car park near the hall (GR 964823). Toilets. Parking charge for non-NT members.
Map OS Explorer OL1 Dark Peak. The Lyme Park complimentary leaflet has a useful map of the park showing all the footpaths.
Refreshments The NT coffee shop is open daily from April to October. There is also a picnic area. Check with www.nationaltrust.org.uk for winter opening hours or telephone 01663 762023.

The Walk

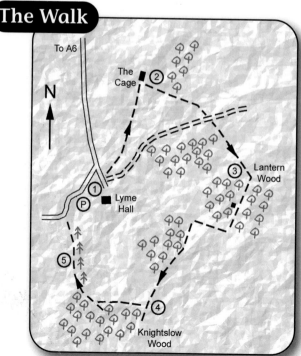

1 From the car park walk towards Lyme Hall and climb the steps. Try counting them; we made it 62. Crossing the track, you continue climbing up the grassy ridge of Cage Hill. From here there's a good view of the planes landing at Ringway.

2 Reaching The Cage, you turn right. A grassy path, good for running down, dips into the valley to the right of the wood and then climbs past the Deer Sanctuary. Crossing the track, continue to a stile then the path heads up the rough pasture to a high ladder stile into Lantern Wood (the nearby Deer Leap may be easier).

The red deer in Lyme Park.

3 A pretty little path leads through the trees above The Lantern to another high ladder stile onto the moor. Turn downhill beside the wall and, staying on the edge of the moor, turn left beside the wall.

4 In about ⅓ mile go through the wooden gate (latch on the other side) and follow the path down beside the Fallow Deer Sanctuary. Crossing the top of the Lime Avenue, you join the path through Knightslow Wood and turn right.

◆ Fun Things to See and Do ◆

Ask the children why **Lyme Cage** only has three sundials not four and is it telling the correct time?

Lantern Wood is a good hide and seek spot. Children enjoy visiting The Lantern, which was built in 1792 and has a vista down the hill to Lyme Hall, but why are there no windows at the back?

The tall **ladder stiles** are great fun to climb and the high walls were built to keep the deer out, so why have they now been given this access to the woodland? (It is to provide grazing and shelter.) Also there are white park cattle and highland cattle, which graze on the longer, coarser grasses.

If you visit **Lyme Hall**, there are hands-on activities for younger visitors and also special celebrations at Christmas, including a visit to Santa Claus. There is also a permanent orienteering course.

5 This leads out into the parkland and descends beside a Scots pine plantation, back to the car park and the children's adventure playground.

◆ Background Notes ◆

A visit to **Lyme Park** is always an enjoyable day out. The stately mansion has rooms decorated and furnished in Elizabethan, Stuart, Georgian and Edwardian times while the gardens are both formal and informal and there is a fine lake. **Lyme Cage** in the grounds was built in the 1520s as a watchtower. It once housed the male servants and was later restored as a viewing point and banqueting house with large doors so horses could be ridden into the ground floor. It is open to the public some weekends.

The 1,400 acres of parkland, woodland and wild moorland are home to both **red and fallow deer**. In 1750 Dr Richard Pocock remarked, 'The great curiosity of this place are the red deer.' That was the year Joseph Watson, the park keeper, died. He had been in the job for 76 years and it must have suited him for he was aged 102. The stags and hinds live in separate groups, except in autumn when they come together at the 'rut'. Their ancestors were part of the Macclesfield Forest herd, and you are almost bound to see some, for Lyme has over 500 of these magnificent creatures. Although there have been fallow deer at Lyme for centuries, the numbers declined after the war and they were reintroduced in 1981. They now graze in a sanctuary, which is open to the public from April to October. **The Lantern** was erected in 1729 on what was then open hillside. The **Lime Avenue** has been a feature of the park since the 17th century and the young trees will take 180 years to grow to their full height.

Legend says that **Knightslow Wood** is named after a crusader, Sir Piers Legh, who was buried here after being fatally wounded at the Battle of Agincourt. His daughter, Blanche, was so distressed that she drowned herself in the River Bollin, and the ghostly White Lady still looks for her father's grave.

9

Alderley Edge

A Wizard Walk

So, where are we?

As sunlight slants through the beech leaves, or autumn mists swirl across the Cheshire Plain, the woods at Alderley Edge have an enchanted air. This is a place of magic and mystery, folklore and fable, where at any moment you might meet a wizard and be shown a cave full of sleeping warriors. Legend tells how King Arthur lies here in a hidden cavern. And, indeed, Alderley Edge really does have caves. Amidst the trees a great gash cuts through the rocks and, on the lip of the Edge itself, a mass of boulders tumbles down the hillside. Copper and lead mines dating back to pre-Roman times, say the experts. Yet who knows, maybe the great leader still sleeps beneath these sandstone cliffs ready to wake in time of England's greatest need.

Kiddiwalks in Cheshire

9

Getting there *Alderley Edge village stands on the A34 about 12 miles south of Manchester. The National Trust car park, and Alderley Edge itself, are 1 mile east on the B5087.*

Length of walk 1½ miles.
Time Up to 2 hours.
Terrain Easy paths, which are navigable by pushchairs.
Warning Both Stormy Point and the Edge have unfenced drops.
Start/Parking The National Trust car park (free for NT members), toilets (GR 859772).
Map OS Explorer 268 Wilmslow, Macclesfield & Congleton.
Refreshments Wizard Tea Room (open Saturday, Sunday and bank holidays) and the Wizard pub. There is a picnic area and often an ice cream van. The County Hotel, 1 mile north of Alderley Edge on the A34, serves food all day and offers Wacky Warehouse indoor play building for kids (telephone: 01625 582294).

The Walk

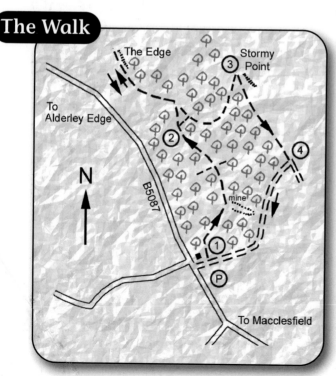

1 Just past the whitewashed NT information centre take the path into the woods then branch right, signed with a pink arrow. This leads past the fenced Engine Vein Mine and you keep straight on at the path junction to the Armada Beacon.

2 (Pushchairs must double back here and follow the main path downhill.) TAKE CARE if you decide to visit the Edge, an out and back the same way route to an unfenced cliff top. Go to the left of the fencing, by the wall, and turn left along the higher path. After admiring the view, retrace your steps and keep straight on along the main path.

3 Reaching the rocky Stormy Point (more unfenced drops), turn

◆ Background Notes ◆

The legend of the **Alderley Edge Wizard** relates that a farmer from Mobberley went to sell his milk-white mare at Macclesfield Fair. On the way he met an old man who told him he would be unable to sell the horse and indeed this was the case. When he returned, the old man, who was in fact a wizard, took him to Alderley Edge where a rock split open to reveal a pair of iron gates. Inside were many sleeping knights and all but one had a milk-white steed. The wizard explained that in times of danger the army would ride out to save the country and one of them needed the farmer's horse. This is thought to be one of the many legends about King Arthur and the Knights of the Round Table.

The **beech and Scots pine** at Alderley Edge were planted around 1779 by Lord Stanley. Before then the area was all open heathland.

The **beacon site** was used in 1588 to signal the coming of the Spanish Armada.

Castle Rock, another wonderful viewpoint, was cleared in 1255 by Ranulph, 6th Earl of Chester. He started to build a castle, then changed his mind and constructed it at Beeston instead. The rock was used as a defence point during the Civil War.

The **Engine Vein Mine**, a deep sandstone cleft now fenced to prevent erosion, is the oldest mine on the Edge and copper has been extracted here since the Bronze Age. Some 38 different minerals have been found. When you've finished your walk, call in at the information centre to look at the various displays and learn more about the mine.

right along the escarpment. Continue beside the fence, then keep straight on and follow the path to the field corner.

4 Go through the gate and turn right to follow the track back past the Engine Vein Mine to the information centre.

◆ Fun Things to See and Do ◆

Before you set off, tell the children the story of the **Alderley Edge legend** and then keep a sharp eye out for wizards on the walk. This is a great place for **hide and seek** but do take care not to let the children run ahead near the Edge and on Stormy Point where there are unfenced cliffs.

The old mine at **Stormy Point** – a splendid viewpoint 600 ft above the Cheshire Plain to the Peak District hills – has a metal grill and could easily be the entrance to the hidden cave where the knights are sleeping. If you walk round this seven times and repeat the Lord's Prayer backwards, the Devil will appear, we are told! This is a fantastic spot for youngsters to explore the deep cleft and scramble on the sandstone rocks. Alan Garner's children's book *The Weirdstone of Brisingamen* is all about Alderley Edge and the wizard legend. It is very exciting and older children will love having this read to them, though perhaps not at bedtime!

The delightful National Trust **Hare Hill Garden** is only a mile away (go south-east along the B5087). The wooded and walled garden has a good display of rhododendrons and azaleas. Open April to October. Telephone: 01625 584412; www.nationaltrust.org.uk

Jodrell Bank Observatory is about 5 miles away, just off the A535 between Holmes Chapel and Alderley Edge. There is a visitor centre and a new observational platform at the base of the telescope. A 3-D theatre lets you journey through the solar system and fly to Mars. Telephone: 01477 571339; www.jb.man.ac.uk

10

White Nancy

A Landmark for Miles Around

White Nancy.

Cheshire is best known for its pastoral landscapes, with cows grazing peacefully in flat green fields. But when the land rears up into a hill, the county excels itself with some worthy summits and memorable skylines. Kerridge Hill is instantly recognisable from the towns of Macclesfield and Bollington to the west and from the Peak District to the east, yet its uniqueness is not the outline, but the eye-dazzling White Nancy. This beehive-shaped monument acts as a beacon, for when you've found the gleam of white on the horizon everything else fits into place. And what a summit cairn it is! Even adults are dwarfed beside it, and even if the whole family join hands they still won't manage to encircle White Nancy.

Kiddiwalks in Cheshire

◆◆◆ *10* ◆◆◆◆◆◆◆◆◆◆◆◆◆◆◆◆◆◆◆◆◆◆◆◆◆◆

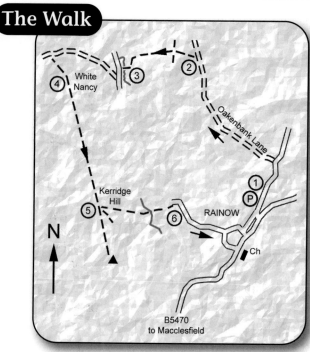

Getting there *Rainow lies between Macclesfield and Whaley Bridge on the B5470.*

Length of walk 3 miles.
Time Allow 3 hours.
Terrain Field footpaths, then a climb with a steep, stepped ascent and a steep descent. The toughest walk in the book and only for experienced Kiddiwalkers who like a challenge.
Start/Parking In Rainow, roadside parking off B5470 on Smithy Lane, past the Robin Hood (GR 953764).
Map Explorer OL 24 White Peak or Explorer 268 Wilmslow, Macclesfield & Congleton.
Refreshments The Robin Hood pub has outside seating or you could picnic anywhere on Kerridge Hill.

❶ Set off along Smithy Lane with views across the valley to Kerridge Hill and White Nancy. Reaching a grassy triangle, fork left and follow the stony bridleway of Oakenbank Lane over the shoulder of High Cliff.

❷ About 200 yards beyond the hilltop a footpath sign points left at a gateway, across the field to join the Gritstone Trail by Ingersley Hall. Now keep a lookout for the yellow 'G' waymark which signs the route. Continue descending beside the wall through a series of wooden kissing gates and under some fine sycamore trees. If you're there at the right time of year, the

The Walk

(map labels: White Nancy, Oakenbank Lane, Kerridge Hill, RAINOW, Ch, N, B5470 to Macclesfield; numbered points 1–6)

children can throw the winged seeds into the air and watch them helicopter to the ground.

3 Reaching the valley bottom, cross the sturdy stone bridge over the River Dean, where one of the surviving mills is off to the right, and turn left along the track. Just before you reach the house the Gritstone Trail doubles back and it is a steady plod uphill past humps of old mine spoil from shallow coalpits. As you reach the highest point of the track a neatly constructed stepped path heads straight up to White Nancy.

4 From the monument you look over to the Cheshire Plain and northwards to Greater Manchester. Now the hard work of the day is done and you head south, following the ridge wall along the Saddle of Kerridge, through yet more kissing gates. Eastwards the views are over the valley to the Peak District hills, then the path crosses to the other side of the wall, above the stone

◆ Fun Things to See and Do ◆

This is lovely Cheshire countryside and Oakenbank Lane is a good spot for blackberrying and picking bilberries in season. On the approach, see how often you can spot White Nancy as the monument plays hide and seek behind the hilltops. The climb to the top is up steep, solid, gritstone steps. One idea for encouraging the children is to turn the climb into a race.

From White Nancy you look down on Bollington and the children can count the chimneys of the old mills, originally built for spinning and weaving. See if you can pick out any distant landmarks like Jodrell Bank or the Welsh Hills. If you live nearby, maybe you can even see your own house.

The second crossing of the River Dean is a good **picnicking and paddling** spot, for either bare feet or wellies.

quarries, and you look down upon Macclesfield.

5 Crossing back over the wall, the Gritstone Trail sets off downhill. (Strong walkers can continue along the ridge for another ¼ mile to visit the trigpoint and return the same way.) Leaving the Trail, you take the lower path, which slants across the field, then heads straight down into the valley. Cross the infant River Dean, then climb a small rise and follow the field edge.

6 Reaching Sugar Lane, turn right into Rainow, then turn left at the T-junction. Chapel Lane leads round to Stocks Lane where you go left again. Then, just before you reach the Robin Hood, look for the village stocks.

◆ Background Notes ◆

The whitewashed folly of **White Nancy**, which shines brightly when there is sunshine, high above the little mill town of Bollington, was erected in 1820 to commemorate victory at the Battle of Waterloo. It was built by the Gaskells who lived at Ingersley Hall, now Savio House, a religious retreat, and is named after a member of their family. From the bell-shaped monument there is a bird's-eye view of Bollington, to the north-east is Lyme Park and on a clear day the South Pennine hills can be seen. Westwards, beyond Jodrell Bank and Alderley Edge, the escarpment of Beeston Castle stands out on the Cheshire Plain, and further still are the Welsh mountains.

Rainow stands on the boundary of the Peak District National Park and its Anglo-Saxon name means Raven's Hill. Stocks Lane was the main route through the village until 1771 when the modern turnpike road was constructed. It is named after the stocks, which have stood here since the 13th century. Rainow was once a busy industrial centre. There were nine water-powered cotton spinning mills on the River Dean, and there was also quarrying and coalmining. The working quarries on the west side of Kerridge Hill have been in existence for hundreds of years, supplying Cheshire with paving stones and roofing slates, but the last coalmine closed in 1926.

11

Tegg's Nose

Gritstone and Machinery

Pausing for a rest.

Where can you find a Jaw Crusher, a Stone Shifter and a Swing Saw? The answer is on Tegg's Nose, high above Macclesfield Forest. Here, in the heart of an old quarry, the machinery has been preserved, while among the piles of discarded gritstone, moorland flowers bloom. Scrambling over this giant Bob the Builder set is great fun for children whatever their age, and from the heathery summit you look down on sunken packhorse ways, once used by smugglers of illicit salt. But who was Tegg and what about his nose? Well, Tegge was an early Norse settler – or perhaps the profile of the hill looks like a 'teg' or young sheep. Certainly its outline is easily identified. Every August gasping fell runners reach the summit the hard way, straight up the front.

Kiddiwalks in Cheshire

11

◆◆◆◆◆◆◆◆◆◆◆◆◆◆◆◆◆◆◆◆◆◆◆◆◆◆◆

Getting there *Tegg's Nose Country Park is 2 miles east of Macclesfield and signed from the A537.*

Length of walk 1 mile.
Time Allow at least 1 hour, with extra time for playing on the old machinery.
Terrain Broad, easy paths with just one narrow section. You could take a pushchair into the Country Park, but it would be hard work in some places on the gritty paths.
Start/Parking Tegg's Nose car park (small charge), toilets (GR 950733).
Map Explorer OL 24 White Peak or Explorer 268 Wilmslow, Macclesfield & Congleton.
Refreshments The car park has a very attractive picnic area, with fabulous views and a coin-operated telescope.

The Walk

❶ From the entrance to Tegg's Nose car park take the broad footpath beside the road. This passes an old milestone, which has the archaic spelling 'ff' in the middle of the word Macclesfield. How far is it to London?

❷ Reaching the Country Park, turn left up big steps not designed for short legs. The path leads through bilberry and heather heathland and soon there is a splendid view across to the wooded slopes of Macclesfield Forest.

3 On entering the old quarry you will see some interesting machinery beside a picnic area. What was the machinery used for? You continue past the big quarry hole where you may see

◆ Fun Things to See and Do ◆

Tegg's Nose Visitor Centre now sports a small wind turbine, which catches the attention as you arrive. There is a notice board explaining why this is a perfect site to demonstrate renewable energy and that the turbine should have paid for itself in about 10 years.

There are many excellent information boards in the Country Park. The ones in the quarry tell how Tegg's Nose gritstone rock was formed 325 million years ago and that there has been quarrying here since the 1500s. There is a good view of the layers of pink millstone grit in the exposed quarry face. The old machinery in the quarry makes a fun place for children to play. They can climb up into the cab of the derrick crane, scramble over the big square swing saw and balance along other bits of machinery, safely only a few inches off the ground.

At the Langley viewpoint, 'A Quarryman's View', above a steep scree slope, you look down on three reservoirs and can identify Shutlingsloe and Croker Hill from the explanatory drawing. The Cheshire viewpoint at 1,246ft, 'From Hill to Horizon', gives a skylark's view across the Cheshire Plain and from here you can pick out the Jodrell Bank telescope and Beeston Castle. To locate Manchester Airport, watch where the aircraft are landing.

The circular stile at the end of point 5 has labelled spy holes, which the children can look through to identify distant landmarks.

If it is snowy, the **Sledging Field** will be full of excited children for this is one of the few places in Cheshire where sledging is actually encouraged.

Kiddiwalks in Cheshire

children learning to climb and abseil.

4 Keeping left, you come to the end of the promontory where a little path goes left to a splendid viewpoint. Return to the main path and continue round the hilltop.

5 Reaching a gate, you turn sharp right, then go left before you reach the next gate and climb the hill to another viewpoint. Continue to an unusual circular stile. What are the holes for?

6 The path then leads along the top edge of the Sledging Field. Next comes the steep slope of an old quarry, a bit more field and finally you join a track, which leads back to the Country Park footpath.

◆ Background Notes ◆

The rocky prow of **Tegg's Nose** rises above Macclesfield, giving extensive views over the Cheshire Plain to the Welsh Hills. The car park is on top of what was once Windyway Quarry, which produced a blue gritstone. The hilltop has been much quarried away, but this only adds to the interest. The heathery mounds as you enter the park are old spoil heaps. Quarrying reached its heyday in the late 1800s and Tegg's Nose was one of the largest quarries in the area, employing up to 20 people, but quarrying ceased in 1955. The pink millstone grit, which is very hard wearing, was used to make paving stones, walling stones, gateposts, troughs and roofing slabs. At first much of the high quality stone was levered out with bars, but from the 1930s crushed stone was needed to build roads and airfields and this was blasted out. There is a Rock Crusher in the old quarry, which could crush up to 100 tons of rock a day, filling five big lorries. In the past, 70% of Macclesfield's streets were paved with Tegg's Nose stone. Information boards tell how the pieces of quarry machinery worked and detail what to look for at the viewpoints.

12

Gawsworth

Beauty and the Bog

Beside the Macclesfield Canal.

Gawsworth, with its 13th-century church and 15th-century half-timbered hall set beside a lake, is as pretty as a picture. So why go to a bog? Well Danes Moss is a nature reserve – it's the largest raised bog in lowland England – and you don't walk on the boggy bits! Even selecting a thoroughly wet day for the outing, as we did recently, does not detract from the experience. We found the fishermen on the lake hunching under their umbrellas as the rain dripped through the trees – but four-year-old Heather romped over the fields, along the canal, across the highest of railway bridges, pretended to be a fox in the undergrowth and finally, despite the now torrential rain, insisted on the promised swings and slides.

Kiddiwalks in Cheshire

12

The Walk

1 Continue along the lane past Gawsworth church and the lake which fronts Gawsworth Hall. Reaching the T-junction, turn right and follow the track past an imposing statue of Lord Peel and by the fishing ponds, with a view across to the early 18th-century Gawsworth New Hall. Then, passing the square Pigeon House, the path continues over grassy fields through a series of metal kissing gates.

2 Reaching Woodhouse End Road, keep straight on past

56

◆ Fun Things to See and Do ◆

A **walk by a canal** is always interesting with lots of activity and boats to wave to as they chug by; most people wave back – especially to children.

Imagine having a canal footbridge erected specially just for you – the one you pass was purpose-built for the occupants of Canal Cottage. Further on there is a swing bridge. Why is this here and how does it work?

Before the **railway footbridge** was constructed, to attempt a crossing of the high-speed main line linking Manchester with Stoke-on-Trent was far too dangerous. Why is the bridge is so high, and how many steps are there?

Children can look for the **old rails** on Danes Moss, half hidden in the grass. The path follows the line of an old horse-drawn tramway, which carried wagons full of peat to the canal. What was the peat used for?

When you enter **Maggoty Wood** let the children go ahead to hunt for the grave (see Background Notes).

The picturesque **Gawsworth Hall** is open to the public and this ancient manor house is well worth a visit. The hall has a wide range of open-air theatre events, some of which are suitable for children. More information on www.gawsworthhall.com or telephone 01260 223456.

Older children will enjoy a visit to the **church** to see the gargoyles on the tower and also the elaborate Fitton graves inside the church. Take some bread to feed the ducks.

Mount Farm and continue over the railway and past Paddock House and Fodens Farm. What is the tower you can see on the hill used for? (Answer: telecommunications.) At the bend, a green footpath sign points left down the track to Woodhouse Green Farm. Waymarks direct you right and round the outbuildings, then the path goes straight down to join the Macclesfield Canal by Canal Cottage.

3 Turn left along the towpath and under the wooden footbridge. Continuing beside a wood, you arrive at swing bridge No 47. Here you turn left and cross the railway over what is certainly the high spot of the walk.

4 Entering Danes Moss Nature Reserve, the path follows the line of an old horse-drawn tramway. The children can look for the rails – they are easiest to see near a stretch of open water. Leaving the moss, the old tree-lined sunken track continues to a junction.

Looking for rails in Danes Moss.

Turn right and another old trackway leads to a stile. Cross the field diagonally, then continue along the field edge to join a farm track.

5 Turn left, then go right at the junction. At the bend a footpath keeps straight on, then a waymark points left along the field edge. Emerging into the houses, turn right, then go left at Gawsworth Primary School and

Gawsworth

right along Woodhouse Lane to a little green. What can you see here? (Pump and stocks.) Now turn left and walk back past the splendid children's playground, which is behind the Scout Hut. Just before the crossroads explore Maggoty Wood and then walk back up Church Lane.

◆ Background Notes ◆

The Fittons built both the half-timbered **Gawsworth Hall** and the church with its eight-spired tower, shields of arms and gargoyles in the 15th century. The family owned the manor for 400 years. This was the home of Mary Fitton who was Maid of Honour to Queen Elizabeth I, but was disgraced when she had a baby, and her ghost has been seen gliding through the church. It has been suggested that Mary was the Dark Lady of Shakespeare's sonnets, so did the bard ever visit Gawsworth? If you meet the ghost you must ask her!

Peat was last cut from **Danes Moss** in 1966 and the raised moss now belongs to the Cheshire Wildlife Trust who have restored the wetland. The area, with its oak and Corsican pine woodlands, has at least six species of sphagnum moss, also cotton grass and cross-leaved heath. There are areas of open water, which attract wildfowl in winter and early spring, while 19 species of butterfly, including the rare hairstreak, and over 30 different moths have been identified.

Samuel 'Maggoty' Johnson lived from 1691 to 1773 and the inscription on his grave in **Maggoty Wood** describes him as 'distinct from other men by the eccentricities of his genius and a wit, musician, poet, player and dance-master'. So called because he was very ugly, Johnson was the last professional court jester in England and worked at Gawsworth Hall. He was determined to be buried in a vault on unconsecrated ground so that his bones would be undisturbed on the day of resurrection but, in 1851, an additional epitaph, which had a more pious tone, was added.

13

Chester Walls

A Walled City

Looking over Eastgate.

H umpty Dumpty sat on the wall, but at Chester you can walk all round the city walls. This is the most complete walled city in England and, since the 18th century, walking the walls has been a popular excursion. Protectively encircled by the River Dee, and with its unique double 'Rows' of shops, topped by fairytale black and white half-timbering, Chester is a delightful city. But it is the red sandstone walls that set it off to perfection. Daniel Defoe thought the walls 'a very pleasant walk', while Henry James claimed to have quite lost his heart to them. Perhaps, though, the Roman sentries thought differently when standing guard at Deva, their fort built nearly 2,000 years ago – they were a long way from home.

The Walk

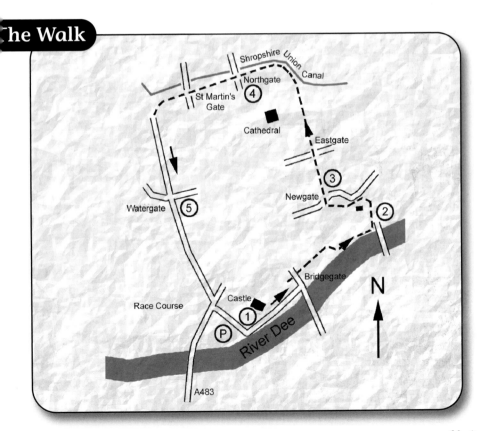

Kiddiwalks in Cheshire

13

Getting there *Though Chester is the capital of Cheshire it stands right on the edge of the county on the Welsh border.*

Length of walk 2 miles.
Time At least 2 hours, but allow a full day to include the other city centre attractions.
Terrain Easy paths but lots of steps; only some sections of the wall are suitable for pushchairs.
Start/Parking We recommend starting at the Little Roodee long stay pay & display car park (where there are toilets) by Grosvenor Bridge, just off the A483 Wrexham road (GR 406657).
Map Chester is on Explorer 266 but the OS map is no help at all for this walk around the city; if possible buy a Chester Walls Walk map, which is available locally, or visit www.chester.gov.uk and download a map.
Refreshments Chester is well supplied with suitable places to eat and you can picnic by the river or in the park.

❶ Crossing Castle Drive, near Grosvenor Bridge you turn right along the city walls beneath the red sandstone ramparts of

Chester Castle. The walk briefly joins the road before climbing back up to the wall at BRIDGEGATE. Continue high above the streets then leave the wall and go down the Recorder's Steps to walk beside the Dee.

❷ At the silver suspension bridge turn left up the steps and past Grosvenor Park, then go left round the gaunt ruins of St John's church to join the road opposite Chester Visitor Centre. Turning left you pass the Roman Amphitheatre and the Roman Garden.

❸ Rejoining the wall at NEWGATE, you continue along the wall to EASTGATE. Chester

The splendid clock towering over Eastgate.

Cathedral now comes into view. Then, passing the grassy expanse of Deanery Fields, you arrive at King Charles's Tower. Next comes a precipitous plunge to the Shropshire Union Canal.

◆ Fun Things to See and Do ◆

The children can do the **route finding** – just join the wall and keep walking. Look out for the metal panels that tell stories about the different parts of the wall. Youngsters can bring paper and crayons to take rubbings of the raised text and illustrations. It is interesting to compare the five gates that lead into the walled city for each has a different character.

The walk leaves the wall to visit the **River Dee**, which has boats, birds and bridges to look at and has the feel of a seaside resort with cafés and ice cream kiosks. The **Queen's Park Suspension Footbridge**, built in 1923, is anchored to the ground by enormous twisted steel cables and if you take a walk over the Dee the children will feel the bridge vibrating beneath their feet.

If you are lucky you will see a fully suited and authentic **Roman Legionary** leading one of the Roman tours round the city, while the Roman Amphitheatre is the site of an archaeological dig.

The most distinctive feature of Chester is **The Rows**. These are double-level walkways with shops at street and first floor level that have been here since the 14th century. Even the children will like shopping here.

After the walk, and the shopping, the children can enjoy a trip on one of the **two showboats**, the Lady Diana and the Mark Twain, which operate up and down the Dee.

Ragamuffins, a large indoor play area for children, is situated on the other side of the river. Telephone: 0845 0066220; www.ragamuffins.co.uk

Kiddiwalks in Cheshire

13

4 Beyond the oldest section of the wall at NORTHGATE you pass Morgan's Mount and cross ST MARTIN'S GATE to Pemberton's Parlour, while outside the walls is the Canal Basin. The wall bends at Bonewaldesthorne's Tower, which is connected by a long spur to the Water Tower, then you descend to the road and continue past the Queen's School to WATERGATE.

5 Continue along Nuns Road, with a grand view of Chester Racecourse, and cross the busy Grosvenor Road back to the river and the car park.

◆ Background Notes ◆

While the streets below are thronging with shoppers, up on the walls you are in a different world. Here is a brief list of things to look out for in the order you pass them, though the metal information panels will tell you much more:

Chester Castle was a medieval stronghold of William the Conqueror. **Bridgegate** stands above the 14th-century Old Dee Bridge and below to the left is the half-timbered 1664 Bear and Billet. The **Roman amphitheatre** is the largest ever found in Britain, while the adjacent small garden contains Roman columns and a hypocaust, which provided underfloor central heating. **Newgate** is modern and below to the right you can see the foundations of the Roman fort. **Eastgate** has a splendid clock dated 1897 and stands high above familiar modern shops, topped with Victorian black and white half-timbering, while looking left you can see the sandstone cross that marks the centre of the city. From **Northgate** you can just see the tiny Bridge of Sighs over which condemned men crossed from prison to chapel. **St Martin's Gate**, built in 1966, is the newest of Chester's gateways and leads over the modern by-pass. **Pemberton's Parlour** has a view of Northgate Locks and the Canal Basin. **Bonewaldesthorne's Tower** originally stood on the river, but as the Dee gradually silted up and edged away, the **Water Tower** was built further out, and is connected by a long spur of wall. The River Dee once came up to **Watergate** and here ships unloaded when Chester was a busy port.

14

Little Budworth Country Park

Woodpeckers Point the Way

How far is it now?

As you walk through the woods at Little Budworth, you can sometimes hear a sound like a hungry wolf. But there are no wild animals lurking in the undergrowth, it's the distant snarl of racing cars. Now everybody's heard of Oulton Park, yet only a few people know about Little Budworth County Park. Cheshire's polo players do though, for close by is the county's number one polo ground, where the crack of mallet on ball and the thunder of hooves echoes through the trees. Getting lost in a wood is often easy, but at Little Budworth Country Park there's no excuse, for the walk is waymarked with carvings of a woodpecker. Budworth is named after a Saxon who owned a clearing in the ancient hunting forest, but whether he played games on horseback is anyone's guess.

Kiddiwalks in Cheshire

14

Length of walk 1½ miles.
Time 1 to 2 hours.
Terrain Easy paths; some may be churned up by horses, which makes pushchair pushing hard work.

Start/Parking Little Budworth Country Park free car park (with toilets) is on the Coach Road near the Oulton Park entrance gates (GR 590654).
Map OS Explorer 267 Northwich & Delamere Forest.
Refreshments Best to take a picnic perhaps, but you pass the Egerton Arms on the way to Little Budworth and the Red Lion is opposite the village church. Both pubs have outdoor seating.

The Walk

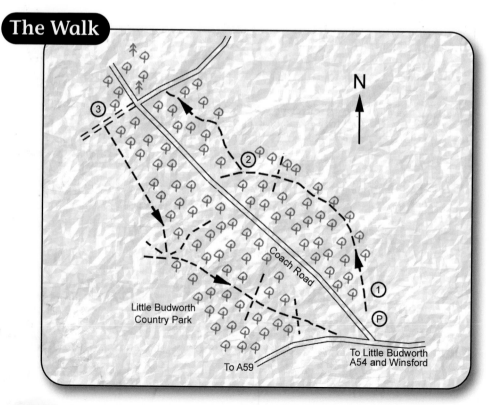

Little Budworth Country Park

❶ The Heathland Trail sets off from the car park past a wooden sculpture – whatever can it be? The path winds its way through the trees and along the edge of the wood. After a gate, you pass Whitehall Moss, the first piece of heathland. Cross a track and continue through the trees, then the Trail forks right.

❷ Passing a pond, where there is a carved seat, a stepped path continues past Beech Moss and by another small patch of heathland. Reaching Beech Road (watch for cars) turn left and keep straight on over the Coach Road.

❸ As you near the edge of the wood, where you can glimpse the

◆ Fun Things to See and Do ◆

The walk follows the **Heathland Trail**. There is a splendid descriptive map board for the children to trace the route at the start and hopefully there should be some free Country Park leaflets. The walk is well waymarked with woodpecker marker posts and youngsters will have great fun hunting for the next purple arrow. How many marker posts do you pass on the walk? There are several wooden seats, made from huge logs, tucked away amongst the trees and the children can identify all the different carved objects.

Many of the tracks are used by horses – look for **horseshoe prints** on the sandy ground. There may be horses on the polo field so listen for the sound of galloping hooves and the clunk of mallet on ball when you reach the edge of the wood. Another sound you may hear is the cars on the **Oulton Park Racing Circuit**. There is lots more buzzing when the heather is in bloom and full of busy bees.

The children can **try to name the trees** in the wood – mostly silver birch, easily identified by its shiny silver bark, which often peels away from the trunk. Then there's the prickly holly and the oak trees with their acorns and wavy edged leaves. These woods are an excellent place to play **hide and seek**.

polo field, a marker points left. The Trail then leads along a strip of woodland beside the heathery heath. When you come to a five-way junction the arrow points on past The Moor, then you keep straight on across another track. Reaching a grassy glade, there are more carved seats to be found, then the Trail crosses Budworth Heath, back to the car park.

Making friends with the dragon.

◆ Background Notes ◆

Little Budworth Country Park is one of the best examples of lowland heath in Cheshire and the paths lead through birch and oak woodland, gorse and bracken, and by colourful patches of heather. Glacial sands were deposited here at the end of the last Ice Age, creating nutrient poor soil ideal for heathland vegetation, and the melting ice formed hollows called kettle holes that are now boggy mires full of sphagnum moss. Most of the park is an SSSI, a Site of Special Scientific Interest.

The first **Oulton Hall** burnt down in 1720 and it was replaced by a large brick mansion, which, some 200 years later, was also destroyed by fire. The Coach Road, which runs through the Country Park, was the 18th-century main drive to the hall. Then, in 1952, the Egerton family leased the park to the firm who owned Brand's Hatch and now **Oulton Park** is famous world wide. Stirling Moss was a five-times winner of the Oulton Park Gold Cup in the 1950s and 60s. The Gold Cup was reinstated in 2002 as a historic event and other highlights of the year include the British Touring Car Championship, the British Superbike Championship and the British F3/GT Championship.

15

Brereton Heath

Woodland and Water

Feeding the ducks at Brereton Heath.

Once a working sand quarry, Brereton Heath has been transformed into a perfect place for an all weather family ramble with small children. With a lake surrounded by trees and encircled by an easy, pushchair-friendly path it would be almost impossible to get lost. But if getting lost is part of the fun then try exploring one of the many little paths that meander off invitingly into the mysterious woodland where a sudden movement among the silver birch trees could be a squirrel, or a blackbird or simply a child playing hide and seek.

Kiddiwalks in Cheshire

15

Getting there *Brereton Heath Country Park is signed from the A54, midway between Congleton and Holmes Chapel. Turn south down Davenport Lane.*

Length of walk 1 mile.
Time Up to 1 hour.

Terrain Broad paths, suitable for pushchairs.
Start/Parking Country Park car park, small charge, toilets (GR 795653).
Map OS Explorer 268 Wilmslow, Macclesfield & Congleton.
Refreshments There may be an ice cream van, if you are lucky.

The Walk

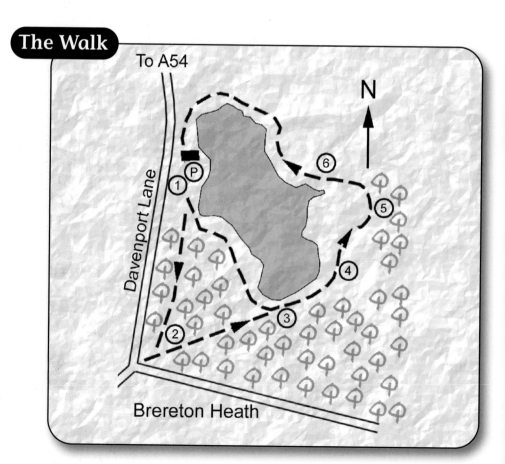

◆ Fun Things to See and Do ◆

Brereton Heath Country Park has an interesting visitor centre, which will tell the children what to look out for on your visit. There will also be details of any special events in the park.

There are many **waterfowl** to identify so be sure and take the binoculars. You should see coots, moorhens and mallards and, possibly, great crested grebes diving for fish, while a family of swans will beg for food. Older children may like to hunt for **wild flowers** so a book could be helpful. The wild flower meadow is full of oxeye daisies, ragged robin and the purple spikes of common spotted orchids. Look for the different **trees** in the woodland; you will find oak, birch, hazel, rowan and holly. Alder grows in the boggy areas and it was used to make clogs and boat keels. Some trees have many trunks and these have been coppiced, that is repeatedly cut down to near the ground, to provide more timber. Local people put food out in the wood so walk quietly and you will see lots of different sorts of tits and other **woodland birds**, but you may also see the great spotted woodpecker, owls and nuthatches, as well as grey squirrels dashing up and down the trees. If you come early in the morning, you may even spot a fox. The woodland ponds have frogs, newts and water boatmen while dragonflies and damselflies helicopter round on sunny days. Can the children tell the difference between the two?

There are **environmental sculptures** around the lake and our favourite is a tunnel made of willow which children love running through. For older children there is a permanent **orienteering course**.

You can also visit **Jodrell Bank Observatory**, which is about 5 miles away (see Walk 9).

Kiddiwalks in Cheshire

15

A good place for a game of hide and seek.

There are no refreshments en route, but lots of handy seats for picnics. Heath Farm, about 3 miles away at Congleton, serves food all day and has Wacky Warehouse indoor play building for children (telephone: 01260 273575). To get there take the A54 to the outskirts of Congleton and then turn right down Box Lane and keep straight on along Padgbury Lane.

1 From the car park take the rightmost path into the trees where yellow-topped posts mark the route. Soon you cross a ditch, which was dug to drain this boggy heathland, and continue through a mixture of oak, birch and coppiced alder.

2 Nearing the edge of the wood, turn left by an impressive sculpture of a red indian in a feathered headdress. The broad path continues through the trees then crosses back over the ditch and leads back to the lakeside path. Here there is a carved post where the children can look for a dragonfly and a mouse.

3 Turn right. The path now follows the wooded lakeshore past a thicket of dogwood which has red branches in the winter. You pass a red box on a post. What do the children think is inside the box? Here reedbeds have been established to provide safe nesting areas for the birds.

4 Continuing round the lake, you pass a lumpy area which is part of the original lowland heath where three types of heather grow. There is ling, bell heather and cross-leaved heath. Can you find all three?

5 Next the path goes through some old Scots pine trees, all that remain of the original Brereton Estate plantation. This is a good spot to play hide and seek and collect fir cones.

6 The lakeside path now goes beside a wild flower meadow, then leads past the information centre, back to the car park. If the children still have some surplus energy, continue on the lakeside path and hunt for the willow tunnel.

◆ Background Notes ◆

This lowland heath of heather and birch trees was once part of the Brereton family estate and was planted with Scots pine in the 19th century to provide timber. Most of the trees were felled during the First World War to provide pit props for coalmining, but a few remain near the lakeshore. Then the land was colonised by silver birch trees and pheasants were reared on the estate and managed by gamekeepers for sport.

In 1959 a very fine, pure silica sand was discovered at Brereton. This was dumped by retreating glaciers at the end of the last Ice Age. For over 10 years the heathland was excavated to supply sand for glass-making, cleaning powders, making moulds for metal casting, and even manufacturing talcum powder. Up to 500 tons were excavated each day and the resulting hole gradually filled up with water. Quarrying ceased in 1972, when the sand was worked out and the area returned to nature, becoming overgrown with scrub. Brereton Heath was purchased by Congleton Borough Council and established as a Country Park in 1982.

In 2004 the Country Park with its 15 acre lake was designated a Local Nature Reserve. Lowland heath is rare in Cheshire and in July and August the heather will be in bloom forming wide purple swathes.

16

The Cloud

A Mountain in Miniature

The wonderful views are worth the climb.

With slopes tinted orange in autumn, snowy white in winter, or a heat-hazy blue in summer, its scarp outline instantly identifies The Cloud. This is everyone's idea of a mountain and though little over a thousand feet, the panorama is finer than from many a hill twice its height. For many local youngsters this is their first proper summit and though recently we carried two-year-old John up in a papoose carrier he insisted on walking every step of the way down and jumping off all the rocks. On the ascent you'll probably meet other children coming down, which adds encouragement, while on the descent there's a wood in which to play hide and seek. Definitely this is a walk where you won't hear that plaintive cry 'How much further is it?'

The Cloud

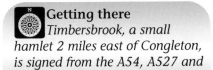 **Getting there**
Timbersbrook, a small hamlet 2 miles east of Congleton, is signed from the A54, A527 and A523

Length of walk 2½ miles.
Time Allow 2 hours.
Terrain After a broad track the ascent is up a rough little path.
Start/Parking Timbersbrook free car park off Weathercock Lane,

◆ Fun Things to See and Do ◆

 A **topograph** details the view from the top of The Cloud so children, with a little help, will enjoy identifying the various landmarks. Mow Cop Folly, Beeston Castle and the white dish of Jodrell Bank radio telescope are easily spotted.

The Cloud summit is excellent for kite flying; it is also popular with model aircraft enthusiasts and even paragliders. Occasionally the gritstone cliffs are used by rock climbers. If you want to explore further then a little path loops round beneath the cliffs. Bilberries grow in abundance on the heathery slopes beneath Cloud Plantation and you can wander off the path to find unfrequented places.

Before you return down the steps to the car park, detour left to look at the **mill pond**, which was built to supply the bleaching and dyeing works with pure, clean water from the Timbers Brook. This water, which tempted the silk industry here during the 18th century, is now regarded as an important breeding site for the common toad.

The National Trust's **Little Moreton Hall**, located 4 miles south of Congleton on the A34, is a medieval moated manor house. It is one of Britain's finest timber-framed manor houses and comes complete with a secret room – always a hit with children. Telephone: 01260 272018; www.nationaltrust.org.uk

toilets (GR 895627). Parking on Tunstall Road, near the end of Gosberryhole Lane, makes the walk easier, with less climbing. Walk up the lane to join the route at point 2.

Map OS Explorer 268 Wilmslow, Macclesfield & Congleton.

Refreshments Take a picnic and have it in the Timbersbrook picnic area or, even better, on the summit of The Cloud where there is a convenient hollow to shelter from the wind.

The Walk

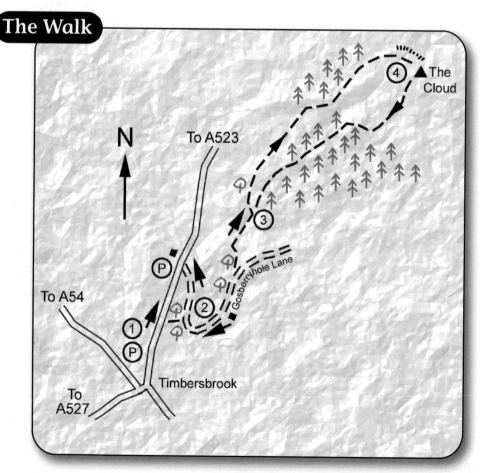

Climbing The Cloud.

❶ From the far end of the Timbersbrook car park continue across the grassy picnic area and climb the steps to Tunstall Road where you turn left. Soon a neatly stepped path climbs through the woodland on the right.

❷ Joining the unsurfaced Gosberryhole Lane, you turn right and continue past Folly Cottage, then at the National Trust sign 'The Cloud' fork left. The stony path leads steeply uphill and, keeping left, suddenly the Cheshire Plain comes into view.

3 Reaching the wood at a stile, take the leftmost path and follow the edge of the plantation. The rough little path continues along the rim of the steep slope and climbs gently through the heather and bilberry.

4 The Cloud summit is topped by an OS trigpoint set on a gritstone plinth. After admiring the view you follow the path down across the heathery moor and into Cloud Plantation, a good place for hide and seek. Then, emerging from the trees at the stile, the outward route is rejoined.

◆ Background Notes ◆

The characteristic scarp shape of **The Cloud** is the best-known skyline in Cheshire and for small children this is an excellent introduction to hill climbing. A topograph commemorating Queen Elizabeth's Golden Jubilee details the view. The summit is edged by steep gritstone cliffs so take care near the unfenced drop. Rock from here was used in 1849 to build the twenty-arched **North Rode railway viaduct** that you can see far below on the Cheshire Plain.

Hidden among the Scots pines of Cloud Plantation are **earth banks**, once thought to be the earthworks of an Iron Age hillfort. But this is still the subject of local controversy and the banks may only be old field boundaries.

The Timbersbrook car park area was the site of the **Silver Springs Bleaching and Dyeing Company**, which was established in the 1900s. The cloth was brought here from Manchester's weaving looms and the factory, which employed 230 people, closed in 1961 and was demolished nine years later.

17

Aldford

A Fairytale Front Door

The magnificent Iron Bridge at Aldford.

Quaint red brick cottages and barley-sugar twist chimneys make Aldford the setting for a fairytale. The village was built by the Duke of Westminster for his estate workers, but when the duke called one day on a local inhabitant the lady failed to recognise her important visitor and told him to come round the back. 'We only use the front door for weddings and funerals,' she told him. 'In that case,' he replied, 'I'll build the rest of the houses without.' The nearby remains of the 12th century motte and bailey castle doesn't have any walls, let alone a door, but much more fun is the Magic Tree. Now that has both a back door and front door – we've been inside!

Kiddiwalks in Cheshire

17

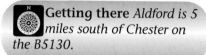

Getting there *Aldford is 5 miles south of Chester on the B5130.*

Length of walk 2½ miles.
Time 2 hours.
Terrain Level, easy walking, though it could be a bit muddy.

Start/Parking Aldford village free car park, opposite the church (GR 420594).
Map OS Explorer 266 Wirral & Chester.
Refreshments The Victorian Grosvenor Arms has an outside terrace and a gate that leads onto the village green – very convenient for the adventure playground.

The Walk

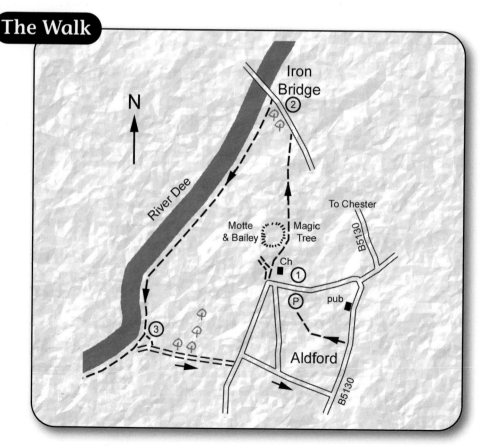

1 Walk out onto Church Lane and turn left. Passing the village hall and the church you then turn right at the T-junction. The footpath keeps straight on, through the white gate and past the earthworks of the motte and bailey fortress and the Magic Tree. The path then continues across the fields, heading towards the distant clock tower of Eaton Hall's Chapel.

2 Reaching the private tarmac drive, you turn left to the magnificent Iron Bridge where a

◆ Fun Things to See and Do ◆

The **Magic Tree** is a hollow oak. It is said that the entrance can close up and keep you prisoner so children have to be very brave to venture inside! Both the acorns and the wavy-edged leaves help identify the tree.

Walk out onto the **Iron Bridge**, which was built in 1824 on the line of the old ford after which Aldford is named. Just imagine what it must have been like to cross this river on foot or horseback, though admittedly the river was a bit lower in those days.

Aldford village has lots of things to look out for. Many of the houses have date stones and all the roads have attractive name plaques. Notice how differently the houses are decorated; some have leaded windows, others are built of brick with blue diamond patterns, there are square, round and twisted chimneys while others have fancy scrolled plaster work and, of course, you must watch for those with no front doors. Look at the house on the corner of School Lane and Rushmere Lane; what are the strange decorations on the gables? The story goes that the grandfather of the present duke thought th the houses he'd built were too plain. After throwing a hu the villagers he used the champagne bottles to d end. You can count how many bottles they dran

To finish off the walk there is a splendid **adventu** the village green.

82

waymark points left, down to the River Dee. The path leads along the field edge beside the broad, tree-lined river, and there are views across to Aldford church with its unusual conical-roofed stair turret.

3 After nearly a mile leave the riverbank and follow the field edge round to a little wooden gate. Turn left up the old green lane, which leads to School Lane where you turn left, then go right on Rushmere Lane. Keeping straight on, you turn left along the main road, then go left again after the Old School House and walk across the village green back to the car park.

Visit the church to see the old bible.

◆ Background Notes ◆

The picture postcard village of **Aldford** gets its name from the old ford where Watling Street, a Roman road, crossed the River Dee into Wales. This was an important defensive point where a grand motte and bailey fortress was constructed in the 12th century. The castle was destroyed during the Civil War then, in the mid 1800s, the village was also destroyed and completely rebuilt by Richard Grosvenor, the 2nd Marquess of Westminster. The village stands on his Eaton estate. The architect for both the houses and the church was John Douglas.

The **church** has a very old bible on the Eagle lectern. There is also an ancient restored sandstone cross in the churchyard.

18

Raw Head

A Walk in the Dark

The Queen's Parlour.

Caves are usually organised places with a ticket office, a guide and lots of lights to show off the features, but at the Queen's Parlour you're on your own. And it's all the better for that. The children will have a lot more fun exploring the blackness with the aid of a torch and who knows what those mysterious shapes in the shadows might be. This cave in the cliffs of Bickerton Hill is reached by a stepped path and was made by locals excavating sand. Pillars of stone were left to support the roof as they tunnelled into the hillside and the further back you go the blacker is the darkness. Occasionally there are special events when there's a storyteller in residence, but usually you'll have it all to yourself. Definitely this will be a day to be remembered. And if you don't fancy caves, the rest of the walk is pretty good too.

Kiddiwalks in Cheshire

18

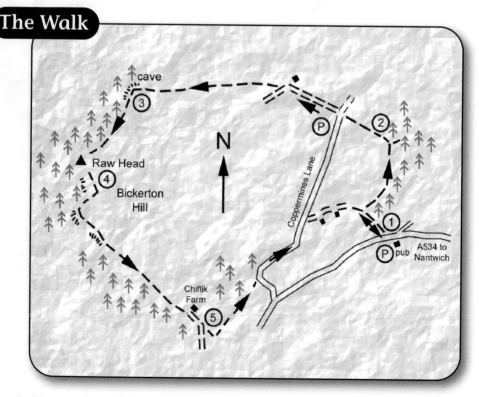

Getting there *The walk starts near the Bickerton Poacher pub, 8 miles west of Nantwich on the A534.*

Length of walk 3 miles.
Time Allow at least 2 hours.
Terrain Good paths most of the way but lots of steps. **Warning** The walk follows the top of a steep sandstone escarpment and there are some unfenced drops.

Start/Parking The Sandstone Trail free car park at the Bickerton Poacher (GR 523544). Roadside parking at the end of Coppermines Lane (GR 521551) makes a shorter, easier walk for younger children – see point 2. **Map** OS Explorer 257 Crewe & Nantwich.
Refreshments The Bickerton Poacher pub welcomes children and has an excellent adventure playground.

The Walk

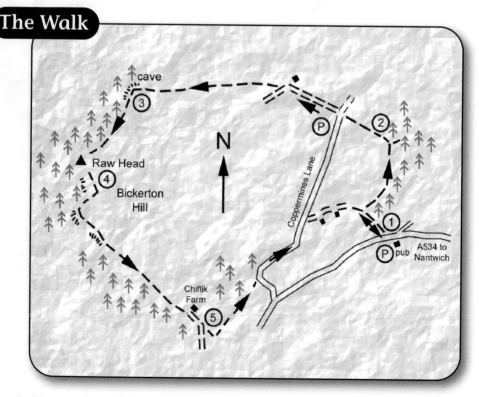

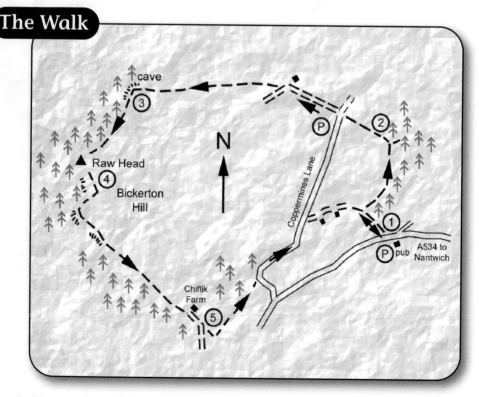

cave

3

N

▲ Raw Head

4

Bickerton Hill

Coppermines Lane

P

2

1

P pub

A534 to Nantwich

Chiflik Farm

5

1 Cross Wrexham Road and take the footpath opposite the Bickerton Poacher which sets off uphill along the field edge. Continuing through the holly trees, you climb to a wooden gate and continue up the old hollow way. At the waymarked junction, turn right along the hillside. The little path leads into the woods of Bulkeley Hill where you turn left to a kissing gate.

2 Joining the Sandstone Trail, the path heads across a field to the end of Coppermines Lane and the alternative starting point. Keep straight on along the broad track until, after The Bungalow, the Trail forks right along the

◆ Fun Things to See and Do ◆

 This is the most exciting walk in the book with a visit to the hidden cavern of the **Queen's Parlour** where children need torches to explore the extensive, shadowy depths. Is the cave natural? Why do the children think it is here? The descent is rather awkward but is well worth the effort. Underground story telling events are held here in the summer months. There is another, more easily accessible cave just below Raw Head.

'**Beneath the Hills**' is an interesting information board, located beside the path beyond Raw Head. It explains the geology of the sandstone cliffs telling how the red rocks, which almost glow in the sun, were formed in a hot desert climate. The iron in the rock was changed by water to red iron oxide so the rocks have really just gone rusty. Looking at the dramatic rich red escarpment you can see where the cliff face has been eroded by wind and rain to form a honeycomb.

Gallantry Bank was the site of a gibbet and here you pass a tall chimney. What is it? The name of the lane gives a good clue.

edge of the escarpment. Continuing through the trees and past gritstone outcrops, you walk above the whitewashed Droppingstone Farm.

❸ At the fence corner steep steps, which can be slippery, lead down to the Queen's Parlour. Return the same way, then continue along the top of the wooded escarpment to the whitewashed trig point on Raw Head.

❹ The stepped path goes above a big scoop in the cliffs to a fenced rocky promontory then continues through the trees to another viewpoint. The Trail then wanders on along the edge and continues beside a field edge to Chiflik Farm. When was the farmhouse built?

The copper mine chimney passed on the walk.

❺ Follow the farm track to the bend where you leave the Sandstone Trail and keep straight on, then turn left. The little path leads across the hillside above Gallantry Bank and past the chimney to join Coppermines Lane. Turn left and after about 350 yards, take the track above Bickerton Hill Cottage. This goes past a house, then tunnels through the holly trees until, reaching the waymarked junction, you turn downhill and retrace your steps to the Bickerton Poacher.

◆ Background Notes ◆

The **Sandstone Trail** is a long-distance footpath linking Frodsham with Grindley Brook near Whitchurch, a distance of 30 miles. Raw Head, at 746 ft above sea level, is the highest point on the Trail.

The **Queen's Parlour** is an artificial cave in the sandstone cliffs referred to on old maps as 'White Sand Hole'. Here local cottagers excavated the fine sand to spread on their cottage floors. There are many caves in the sandstone escarpment and folklore has woven stories around Cheshire's Wild West. One tells of dreadful brigands living in Bloody Bones Cave on Raw Head who terrorised the neighbourhood. The **Droppingstone** is an overhanging rock just beyond the Queen's Parlour after which the farm below is named. There is also a well above the farm where water trickles from the porous sandstone.

The tall chimney is the flue of a pumping engine at a **disused copper mine**. Copper was discovered here in 1697 by Herr Brandshagen, a German engineer, who found that there were already five shafts. He restarted the mining and drew up a list of rules. 'If ye steward should order any miner after their duty hours to any other work, they must obey, or else be punished.' Those were the good old days. The mine buildings were demolished around 80 years ago.

The hollow way used at the beginning and the end of the walk is an old **salters' way** used by salt traders coming from Nantwich into Wales.

19

Maiden Castle

The Final Frontier

Looking over the Cheshire Plain.

The heather-clad escarpment of Bickerton Hill, with a bird's-eye view and precipitous sandstone cliffs facing west almost on the border with Wales, looks ideally suited for defence against Celtic invaders. So finding Maiden Castle on the very edge comes as no surprise. What is unexpected though is that this double row of ramparts and ditch was built long before the Welsh tribes attacked and hundreds of years before the Romans came. Once there were huts with families living here, ever watchful for their enemies until, in 400 BC, all was destroyed by fire. Was it a battle that brought the end, or a dreadful accident? No one knows for sure, but the woods and the bracken covered mounds are a great place for children's mock battles.

Maiden Castle

◆◆

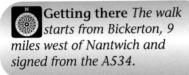 **Getting there** *The walk starts from Bickerton, 9 miles west of Nantwich and signed from the A534.*

Length of walk 1½ miles.
Time Allow a good hour.
Terrain Clear paths through woodland.
Start/Parking Turn down Goldford Lane, by Bickerton's Holy Trinity church, and go right by the pool, opposite Pool Farm. The unsurfaced track leads past the National Trust's Bickerton Hill sign to Pool Lane free car park (GR 503531).
Map OS Explorer 257 Crewe & Nantwich.
Refreshments Take a picnic or visit the child-friendly Bickerton Poacher, the starting point for Walk 18.

The Walk

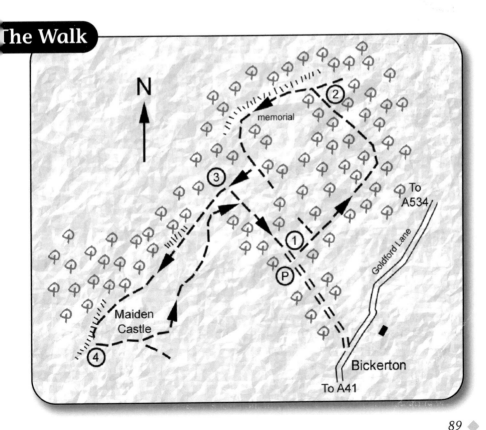

Kiddiwalks in Cheshire

1 Turn right out of Pool Lane car park and follow the stepped sandy path uphill. Keep straight on at the junction and take the obvious path, which wanders through the trees to the right of an open field. Don't go through the kissing gate but follow the black arrows along a path, which loops left by a newly felled area. This is a good spot for hide and seek.

2 Reaching the escarpment edge, turn left along the Sandstone Trail. Next you pass a

◆ Fun Things to See and Do ◆

The highlight of this walk is **Maiden Castle**. An explanatory board tells you about the Iron Age hillfort and there is an illustration to show how the hilltop would have looked when the fort was occupied. With the help of this plan, children can explore the ramparts and find the inturned entrance. What has changed in the view to the west over the last 2,000 years and what still looks the same? Can you pick out the villages that still stand on the tops of the lower sandstone outcrops?

There is an **unusual memorial** to Kitty, wife of Leslie Wheeldon, who gave the land in her memory. There are poems to read, while a photo of Kitty herself overlooks the view.

In the wood there are trees to identify and **birds and butterflies** (in summer) to watch, while Bickerton Hill is great for bilberries. All three types of British heather grow here, ling, bell heather and cross-leaved heath.

The **Candle Workshops** at Burwardsley are only 3 miles to the north of Bickerton, signed from A534. Here you can watch candles being made, and children can have a go in the workshop or visit the play area; there is also a café.

memorial to Kitty, set on a rocky belvedere that gives fine views of the Welsh mountains. Continuing past a Sandstone Trail signpost the Trail goes down a path in a broad sandy cutting to another signpost. The bright orange colour of the rock is due to iron oxide, commonly called rust!

3 Staying on the Trail, you fork right, up a flight of steps, and continue climbing through the trees to the highest point of Bickerton Hill. This flat, bilberry and bracken covered area, is the site of Maiden Castle, an Iron Age hillfort.

On the ramparts of Maiden Castle.

4 After studying the information board and exploring the hillfort, leave the Sandstone Trail and turn left. The path goes to the right of the ramparts, then, in about 100 yards, you fork left on a minor path. This leads across the restored heathland past boggy pools and scattered silver birch trees. Entering the trees, the path becomes more obvious, finally going down a deep cutting. Then, forking right, you head back to Pool Lane car park.

◆◆◆19◆◆◆◆◆◆◆◆◆◆◆◆◆◆◆◆◆◆◆◆◆◆◆◆◆◆◆◆◆◆◆◆◆◆◆◆

◆ Background Notes ◆

Maiden Castle, a name it shares with several other Iron Age hillforts in England, stands at the highest point of Bickerton Hill. The fort was built in about 600 BC, a date determined from the age of timbers found on the site, and it is defended by the natural sheer cliff and two semicircular earth and timber ramparts divided by a ditch. The ramparts can clearly be seen, though they become covered with bracken in the summer. The fort was destroyed by fire around 400 BC, though the area was probably inhabited until the time of the Roman invasion. There are splendid views over the valley of the River Dee.

Bickerton Hill is one of the few lowland heath sites remaining in Cheshire. It is managed by the National Trust who acquired the land with the help of funding from Leslie Wheeldon in memory of his wife Kitty 'so that others may enjoy these Cheshire Hills as much as she did'. In 1992 the Trust began a restoration programme to remove the encroaching trees and to restore the hill to heathland, which is now maintained by grazing Welsh Black cattle. The walk passes a recently felled area where piles of silver birch logs have been left to create mini habitats for birds, animals and insects. There are ravens, buzzards, sparrowhawks and kestrels, the latter easily identified as they hover above the edge, as well as merlins and peregrine falcons, while among the trees are long-tailed tits, nuthatches, treecreepers and woodpeckers. Experts have also identified adders, slow-worms and the common lizard – the latter may be common, but are only glimpsed for an instant in the undergrowth.

For a note on the **Sandstone Trail** see Walks 3 and 18.

20
Audlem

Locks Galore

The Shropshire Union Canal.

With gaily painted boats chugging up and down the canal and tackling the locks, there's always something going on at Audlem. However, we hadn't expected to see a coal boat. Taking a break, its owner relaxed on the towpath while holidaymakers negotiated the flight of locks that drop the Shropshire Union Canal from Shropshire into Cheshire. Now a walk beside a canal will appeal to children of all ages (and less energetic adults, too) as, apart from the locks, it's flat. We used to call our younger son 'The Hill Detector' as whenever the path began to climb his pace slowed to a crawl. So which way does this walk go? Downhill, of course!

Kiddiwalks in Cheshire

20

Getting there *Audlem village is 6 miles south of Nantwich, at the junction of the A529 with the A525.*

Length of walk 1½ miles.
Time Up to 2 hours.
Terrain Footpaths and canal towpath, but only the canal towpath is suitable for pushchairs.

Start/Parking Free car park on the A529 on the Nantwich side of the village, toilets (GR 659437).
Map OS Explorer 257 Crewe & Nantwich.
Refreshments The Bridge Inn and the Shroppie Fly, which has plenty of outdoor canalside seating. There is also a coffee shop in the village. The walk is well provided with picnic tables.

The Walk

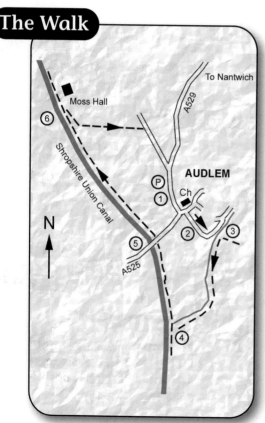

❶ Turn right out of Audlem car park and walk into the centre of the village. Here you will find St Mary's church, a memorial lamp, an ancient buttercross and a bear baiting stone.

❷ Continue down Vicarage Lane past the Old Priest House, now a coffee shop, to Audlem Green and the 1655 Grammar School. Ask the children to look for Rose Cottage, Audlem's smallest house.

❸ Cross the little green-railed, hump-backed bridge and turn right beside the brook (take care above the drop) into Audlem Vale. The path now leads through the meadows beside Audlem Brook, which is overhung with willow and alder. After crossing a footbridge the path climbs to the Shropshire Union Canal.

4 The canal is joined at Lock 11 where you turn right. Strolling along the towpath and down the flight of locks, you pass moored canal boats, many of them brightly painted and decorated.

5 After passing under Bridge 78, which carries the main road into Audlem, you come to the Bridge Inn and the Shroppie Fly. Kingsboro Corn Mill is now a craft shop with good examples of

◆ Fun Things to See and Do ◆

In the centre of Audlem look for the **bear stone** at the far end of the buttercross, which provided shelter for farmers selling butter and cheese. There is an explanatory plaque telling how a bear was chained here to an iron ring so that dogs could cruelly bait it for sport. The stone was originally in the middle of the square. On a more cheerful note you can admire the statue commemorating **Richard Baker Bellyse**, a much-loved doctor who practised in Audlem for 40 years: 'In appreciation of a life spent in relieving the sufferings of his fellow creatures.'

There is lots of interest on the **canal**. Try and choose a sunny weekend when it will be a hive of activity. Watching the narrowboats negotiate the locks is great fun, you may even be able to lend a hand, but do keep your eye on the children as the locks are deep and dangerous. Each lock has a number to hunt for and you can count how many you pass on the walk. Also each boat has a name, fun for older children who are learning to read. The bridges are protected with strips of iron. You can see where the towropes have worn this away when the barges were pulled by horses. The piles of stop planks by the locks are used to block off the canal so it can be emptied for maintenance. Near Kingsboro Mill there is an interesting information board showing what **Audlem Wharf** was like around the 1920s.

painted canal ware. Next you go by a lock-keeper's cottage, which commands an excellent view of the boats approaching from both Cheshire and Shropshire.

6 Just before the last lock, 15, double back and climb up the canal bank, then follow the path across the fields. This goes near the grand Moss Hall, an Elizabethan timber-framed manor house. Then, joining the tarmac lane, walk into Audlem, turning right on the main road, back to the car park.

◆ Background Notes ◆

Three roads meet in the centre of **Audlem**, each named after the county it leads to. This is the most southerly township in Cheshire, set in the midst of dairy farming country. A market charter was granted by Edward I in 1295 and the buttercross was erected in 1733. The 13th-century church of St James the Great dominates the centre of the village. The lovely old Grammar School, a gabled Stuart-style building, was built in the 1650s and remained a school for over 300 years.

At Audlem the **Shropshire Union Canal,** which was built by Thomas Telford in the 1830s, descends from Shropshire into Cheshire. There is a flight of 15 locks, which drop 93 ft in $1\frac{1}{4}$ miles. The waterway, which connected Wolverhampton with Nantwich, took only 8 years to complete.

The **Bridge Inn** was purpose-built as a canal tavern in the 1830s providing stabling for horses, but the **Shroppie Fly**, formerly a warehouse, was made into a public house in the 1970s. A 'fly' was a fast passenger boat which took precedence over all other canal traffic.

Kingsboro Mill, built in 1916, was powered by oil, producing grain and animal feed and has retained its original appearance.

During the Civil War, in May 1644, a battle took place near **Moss Hall** in which the Cavaliers defeated the Roundheads, unlike nearby Nantwich where the Roundheads won.